# Corporate
## *Romance*

By Leslie Aldridge Westoff

*Breaking Out of the Middle Age Trap* (1980)
*The Second Time Around: Remarriage in America* (1977)
*From Now to Zero: Fertility, Contraception, and Abortion
in America*, with Charles F. Westoff (1971)

# Corporate
# *Romance*

### How to Avoid It,
### Live Through It, or Make It
### Work for You

by

## *Leslie Aldridge Westoff*

**Times**
BOOKS

Published in the United States by Times Books, a division
of Random House, Inc.,
New York, and simultaneously in Canada by Random House
of Canada Limited, Toronto.

Library of Congress Cataloging-in-Publication Data
Westoff, Leslie Aldridge.
    Corporate romance.
    1. Women executives.  2. Executives—Sexual behavior.
3. Corporate culture.  4. Organizational change.
I. Title.
HD6054.3.W47     1985      658.4'095      85–40284
ISBN 0–8129–1257–8

Manufactured in the United States of America
9 8 7 6 5 4 3 2
First Edition

**FOR MY MOTHER**

on her eighty-fifth birthday

*Born too soon to become the fine executive
she could have been*

# CONTENTS

# CONTENTS

## Part Two THE SOLUTION

# CONTENTS

# INTRODUCTION

$\mathscr{W}$hen women began to enter the executive suites, the big concern was whether or not they would receive equal pay for equal or equivalent work. It is still an issue. They also worried about whether there would be equal opportunity to be promoted. This too is still an issue. But what nobody seemed to realize was that opening the executive ranks to women was equivalent to an act as monumental as desegregating the South. Women, like blacks in the South, were going to be seen where they never were seen before. And they presumably would work their way up to the various echelons of management, achieving the same social status as their male colleagues who, only recently, had been the sole members of the business fraternity. There was going to be a profound change in the entire sociological structure with which we all grew up and in which we were taught to believe. With both men and women choosing careers in corporations, sexual, family, and business roles would no longer be what they had been.

But monumental changes do not take place easily. When there is preparation, there is less upheaval. Yet there were few people in corporate life who understood that some groundwork had to be laid. No one had prepared. Men had to suddenly face a new reality and change their ways, although they did not want to. And with no one to help, they had to learn how to manage their new male-female business relationships.

What business neglected to see was that although male and female roles were changing, the sexual attraction men and women inevitably feel for each other was still going to be the same. No one had prepared for that, either.

In the course of researching this book, I heard many varied stories from women who work about what happened when romance became part of their business lives. Some stories were happy, but more often they were tales of hurt, horror, and mismanagement. It was evident to me that business was in the middle of a serious culture shock, and no one had called in the organizational behavior counselors to help explain what was going on. Business people needed to learn to relate to the other sex in a new and different way.

It seemed important that sexual attraction in the workplace be examined, reported on, and understood before the situation got out of hand. With new values being imposed on them, with no acknowledgment or direction from the top officers, men could react only with confusion, leaving women equally confused. In such turmoil, corporations could not be expected to function profitably.

This book is meant as both a report on a new phenomenon and a warning to business that certain basic facts of life exist, that little or nothing has been done to recognize and deal with them, and that time is short. If they don't make some changes soon, businesses will find themselves with a problem that will be expensive and awkward to solve. Romance between corporate executives is becoming more and more common, and it is a serious subject. Corporate romance can be devastatingly harmful when not properly managed. A new way of looking at our old notions of male-female relationships must be found. Men and women cannot look at each other in the same way any longer, or respond merely instinctively. Nor can romance be banned, as some corporations are trying to do. Top management cannot continue to count on its human resources as though they were a predictable, unassertive commodity. Business in the mid-1980s has to be viewed with a fresh eye.

# INTRODUCTION

To begin my inquiry, I interviewed executives from many corporations in several parts of the country. Though all were willing to talk, almost all extracted a promise from me that neither their names nor those of their corporations would be used. Such concern about secrecy at times reminded me of movie versions of the terror-inspired, evasive tactics employed by people hiding from the secret police of repressive governments. Nevertheless, believing in the importance of the subject, men and women in major corporations did confide in me. The people, the problems, the anxieties are all real. Actual names have been used only with permission, or in cases from the public records.

The purpose of this book, then, is to analyze the new phenomenon of corporate romance, to ascertain when you can have an affair and when you can't, to see why some office affairs work and some don't, to examine the new pressures and tensions on everyone involved, to document the utter confusion in the rules governing corporate life, to point out the errors that both sides are making, and to suggest what should be done in the future to intelligently manage this very real and growing business development.

*L. A. W.*
*Princeton, N.J.*
*April 1985*

# Part 1

## THE PROBLEM

# Chapter 1

## FACING A NEW PHENOMENON

$\mathcal{T}$he 1984 Democratic National Convention underscored, with the boldest stroke yet, that something new is taking place in the United States. The nomination of a woman exposed a variety of concerns that are by no means limited to politics. People have been wondering, ever since women began entering the work force in masses, precisely how women would be perceived—what their roles would be in the corporation. And the U.S. government is nothing if not this country's largest and most powerful corporation.

When it was just a matter of men candidates relating to other men candidates, no one worried about propriety. No one was concerned with gender-related behavior. The public could listen and look, and any perceptions they had or conclusions they drew were strictly political or a cursory scoring of the candidate's charisma points.

For the first time in this country, a male presidential candidate, Walter Mondale, and a female vice-presidential nominee, Geraldine Ferraro, stood together on the podium. Their advisors handed down papers, not only on ideological positions, but on actual physical positions. Policies were issued on where the two candidates could stand, whether they could touch, whether they could kiss, and what their body language could express to a sexually oriented public.

Newspapers began writing about a new "Etiquette Gap," and everyone from Democratic poll takers and campaign consultants to national political correspondents voiced opinions on how Mondale and Ferraro had to behave toward each other. If they made a wrong move, literally, their chances of winning the election could go down the drain.

Their advisors told them that they had to strike a balance between being friends and being professionals. It was imperative to project the image of being a team rather than a couple because "couples" imply "romance" in the public mind. Romance means sex, and no candidate could win on a sexually tainted ticket.

Therefore, convention watchers saw that when the two candidates stood side by side on the podium, there were no touches or hugs. Male candidates usually hug with one arm and wave with the other, a technique called the "hug-wave mode," and they traditionally raise their clasped hands together in victorious unity. But Mondale and Ferraro were instructed not only just to wave, but to wave with their outside arms so they would not accidentally collide in midair.

Although Mondale hugged and kissed several women at a San Francisco fund-raising event, he was careful not to touch Ferraro. After Mondale and Ferraro were nominated, he kissed Governor Martha Layne Collins of Kentucky and several other women, and Ferraro kissed Jim Wright, the House majority leader, but they were scrupulous about never kissing each other. Absolutely nothing could be construed as sexual.

Political consultant Frank Mankiewicz commented in *The New York Times:* "It's a tough issue that is deep in the collective unconscious. They'll have to go slowly. Their spouses should always be present. They don't want people to think they're ever alone together. They can't touch. They'll have to stay separate for a while."

The monitoring of body language became a campaign issue, as did the checking of speeches to be sure there were no double entendres, which in this new context would leave the candidates open to off-color jokes, laughter, and derision. The presidential and vice-presidential nominee could never talk of their "intimate relationship," as other candidates have done. They could not mention the "broad appeal" that their ticket had. It was suggested that they not even refer to the other person as their "running mate." How they were perceived, in sexual terms, became a political concern for the first time in U.S. history. The top male political offices in the land became coed overnight, and the campaign to win them by capturing the family vote had all the same potential pitfalls as being labeled an X-rated movie.

What is this mysterious, provocative thing that we collectively respond to that so often makes people see normal "asexual" behavior in sexual terms? According to Dr. Norman B. Levy, professor of psychiatry at New York Medical College, one doesn't need a psychiatrist to answer that question. "My illiterate grandmother could tell you about that," he laughed. "She would say that when you have a man and a woman together, although the chances of their making love might be remote," said Dr. Levy, "people spend a good deal of time thinking sexually, because it's one of the nice speculations in life, and this sexual preoccupation engenders fantasies, which we may project onto the people around us."

Human resource consultant Arleen LaBella, cofounder of Resources, Incorporated, in Vienna, Virginia, believes we jump to conclusions about sexual activities at the mere sight of a male and a female because we "don't have any models to understand men's and women's relationships to one another except in terms of sexual alliances. It's rare for men and women to have close friendships without people thinking it must be a sexual attraction. People are not yet able to put it in a context of what it really means, so we put it in a context that is familiar to us."

We make the naive assumption that any man and woman seen together often are a couple. This is felt even more strongly in business, where the likelihood of scandal is far greater now that many more women have been placed in positions of authority. Unfortunately, there are few advisors standing behind the scenes to guide them and their companies through the complex problems that are appearing with alarming frequency.

Consider the following story: not long ago a chief executive officer of a prestigious Midwestern corporation fell in love with a woman in his company. It was especially exciting to him. Married for many years, he had long since ceased to be romantically stimulated by his wife, and had never known anyone else sexually.

He began to take the most foolish risks. They made love in his office. They left notes for each other hidden in public places on company grounds. They met at his lakeside vacation cottage when his family was in the city. One day his wife found them kissing when she came to call for him at the office, and she threatened to leave him and disclose his behavior.

The couple was so indiscreet that before long many people knew of the affair and were shocked that he would risk the reputation of his corporation. They began to question his judgment and occasionally his sanity. They hoped that nothing would happen to harm the company and send its stock plunging. The matter was eventually taken to the Board of Directors, and the chairman spoke to the man. He said he was trying to end the affair, but he needed some time. Later, he and his wife began going to a psychiatrist. But the affair continued. The woman finally left the company and gave him an ultimatum. It pained him, but he decided to stop seeing her and chose to stay with his job and his family. The corporation came within a hairsbreadth of losing its hard-won esteem as well as its top executive, and becoming totally demoralized or even ruined because of a CEO's fancy.

Whether they realize it or not, and most prefer not to, America's corporations are in the beginning stages of an alarmingly disruptive development. Sexual attraction in the office can make or break careers, hurt the corporate image, and cost thousands of dollars in lowered morale, loss of productivity, embarrassing court cases, and the firing of once-valuable employees. But more and more often these enlightened employees are challenging antiquated company rules and norms. Both corporations and executive couples are equally uncertain about how to handle an office romance, and the situation has begun to cause unexpected waves in the once-calm territorial waters of the all-male corporate domain. Business has been so busy trying to obey federal guidelines, accepting women and promoting them into the higher ranks, that it has failed to pause long enough to assess the ramifications of the executive female presence.

Today, 54 percent of all women are in the work force, and the number keeps rising every year. By 1995, the figure will be as high as 65 percent. And in 1981–82, the latest year for which figures are available, almost 30 percent of the business and management graduates of the 544 institutions granting master's degrees were women, according to James A. Viehland, associate director of the American Assembly of Collegiate Schools of Business. Each June this army of female MBAs (today probably more than 20,000) sweeps into corporate jobs that will lead them into executive offices of their very own.

Women hold management positions in increasing numbers. There are already three million in positions of influence. According to the Department of Labor, in 1983 one third of managers, professionals, executives, and administrators were women. Men and women for the first time are working together in large numbers as peers, and they are causing a striking and sudden change in corporate morality.

For one thing, they are breaking the rules of many corporations by fraternizing. They have affairs that turn into marriage, and affairs that break up. Even if a couple were to try to obey every rule, written or unwritten, the extreme mental anguish that could result would not be in the corporation's best interest. The whole situation makes business nervous because when the romantic involvements of male and female executives in a corporation become unmanageable, they shake the foundations of the organization itself. Nevertheless, in reality, there is nothing the corporation can do about it, short of firing the "wrongdoers."

# CORPORATE ROMANCE

In the past, when men and women graduated from college, *he* began his career. *She* married and removed herself to the suburbs to raise a family or took an interim job as a secretary—until the right man came along for her to marry. The man's career in business became his life. He occasionally had affairs, but they did not involve power and did not affect the functioning of the corporation. Above the level of clerks and secretaries, the corporation remained male.

Then, in the 1960s, when the feminist movement began to exert its influence, government rules about sex discrimination were enforced. Nearly a decade later, with increasing demands for sexual equality and a declining college enrollment, the hallowed halls of Ivy League schools opened their doors to women. The prestigious business schools followed suit, and the university, more than ever, became a breeding ground for sex. Coed dormitories sprang up, and sex among students was taken for granted.

Now women's strong interest in careers in business is shifting the grounds for romance into the corporate arena, where it will have a basic impact on the corporate entity. The decision-making process and the fundamental life and health of the organization are affected in ways that never could have happened in the boss-secretary liaisons of the past. With both players in the management hierarchy, the stakes are bigger, and who wins and who loses is not easily predictable.

One of the things that occur when a male and female executive develop a romantic relationship is that they take over more managerial turf than the two would have had separately. Thus they distort the power structure. This causes anger, jealousy, and major disruption among the other executives. They are not so much concerned with questions of morality. It is the loss of power that riles.

In addition to the personal loss, any shift in power has large organizational repercussions. Any change in the established relationships, observes Kaleel Jamison, a Cincinnati management

8

consultant, "especially a change with strong emotional overtones, presents the possibility that the power hierarchy, which is dedicated to efficient production, will crumble." She points out that it is the corporation's structure that makes productivity possible, and that if you strike at the ordained authority connections, you may affect the financial survival of the organization. The male business establishment does not know how to cope with the complex emotions that are being stirred up.

*How should men and women relate to each other in business? How are these female intruders viewed in that once all-male world?*

There are a number of competing tensions. There is the newness of women in powerful management positions, their appearance for the first time in numbers as anything but secretaries. Add to that sexual attractions. Then overlay the unique culture of each organization, the attitudes of top management and that of each particular manager and supervisor, and you have a complex mix of strong personal elements, potential problems, and decidedly volatile ingredients.

Roy Pollack, executive vice president of RCA, voiced the feelings of many men who for the first time are working with high-level women: "I don't have trouble accepting women at work," he said. "I was exposed from the time I was a child to intelligent, capable, self-confident women. If a woman has a good idea, I'll say so.

"On the other hand, I don't mix my social and business lives. That would be devastating. As soon as a woman uses sex toward me, I brush it off. But there are bad effects for her. I worry about how independent her judgment can be. A very bright woman senior executive suggested she meet me for dinner. She was very obvious about it and made the offer a number of times. I decided I wouldn't go near her. At business, I'm all business. If she'd do that with me, she'd do it with others.

"I don't have illusions. I'm fifty-seven and look fifty-seven. I'm losing my hair, I'm overweight, I'm no Clark Gable. She either wanted to get ahead, or get something to hold over my head. I wouldn't take the risk. In the past I have been attracted to women, but my good judgment has come to the rescue."

He believes that the way a man will behave depends on his background, his position, how threatened he feels. "Today men are frightened," he says, "and the present economic situation makes it far worse. Women threaten men economically, and they threaten them with their egos. Men are terrified of being inadequate, rejected, humiliated, diminished because of them."

## THE LAGGING SHIFT IN ATTITUDES

For men and women executives to be able to work effectively together, there must be a change in the way men perceive the other sex. They must be mentally able to understand, accept, and enjoy them as business colleagues. To do this, men will have to resist the temptation, ingrained through centuries of history, literature, and social custom, to compartmentalize women and limit them to certain familiar roles. Even though women are now functioning members of the executive business fraternity, they have not been granted membership cards. It is hard for men to willingly share the powers of running their once exclusive club. It is hard for them to recognize women as professional equals or even superiors. Men are seriously lagging in the need to confront the ways this revolutionary social change affects them. Corporate officers cannot just add women and expect everything to function as it did before. There are attitudes to be altered. Even among those who try, it does not happen easily.

As Janice Eddy, president of Janice Eddy, Inc., a management consultant firm in Kittery Point, Maine, sees it, there are two main issues that always exist between men and women. One is the question of who is in charge, the power issue. The second is the issue of attraction and rejection. "A lot of men's behavior toward women in corporations these days consists of frequently walking on eggshells. Men are afraid of doing and saying the wrong thing and being rejected by a woman or being accused of sexual harassment." Thus they try to change their behavior to accommodate women. But the change is often only superficial, just for the sake of appearance. "I call it wax buildup," says Eddy. "It's adding another layer of new behavior without changing anything underneath."

She finds that some men say, "We'll do the minimum of what is required with women and not much else." They don't really want to change their behavior or get to know women. "I've seen men who've had some of the better records of interacting with women. Yet some leave and go to less liberated companies, admitting that they went along with new corporate policies because they had to, but were enraged by them."

She believes that men are not only afraid of women, but also angry with them, because their presence makes men have to worry about things they never were concerned with before. "It disrupts the equilibrium of the way men do things together. Men alone don't worry about being rejected or harassing one another."

Many men like RCA's Pollack view their rapport with women cautiously. The sexual myths that men perpetuate and that many women buy cause much of the confusion. The man is aggressive, firm, dominant, problem-solving; the woman is emotional, dependent, warm, and temperamentally unfit for management, a seductress to be feared and avoided—we've heard all this before and, by now, realize that it's hogwash. When composites of successful women executives are drawn, they turn out to be just like their male counterparts: independent, tough, ambitious, with the same high needs for dominance and achievement.

The executive vice president of a major advertising firm remarked that "you see a new breed of women in business that you probably didn't see ten years ago. She has many of the same qualities as the male. She wants to build a career. She's not there looking for a husband, and she'll do everything men have tradi-

11

tionally done in corporate settings to grow within the organization." He found some women too aggressive—"There are some real sharks out there"—but he acknowledged that men could be and have been sharks, too; it is just scary because men never saw that in women before. Yet the sexual stereotypes are still strong and get in the way. A woman trying to deal with a man colleague-to-colleague often finds that he retreats to a male-female interaction. As one executive put it, "A woman is going to be looked upon as a woman first, and as an equal human being second, by many, many men for many, many years to come. And it's going to be very difficult for her, especially if she is attractive. It's not going to be solved very easily."

These antiquated stereotypes that hang on despite the lack of justification for them often cause resentment in men which may take a sexual form. Some men may consciously or unconsciously make passes at women simply to demean them, make them less of a threat, and/or keep them in their places as objects of carnal desire. They may continue to try to achieve sexual conquests. Women may fall into the pattern of using their sex to get ahead, as many men expect them to. Different reactions to this sexual tension among executives and the confusion among couples and corporations about how far they can go is causing some knotty situations. On the one hand are the young MBAs continuing the mating game they once enjoyed in college and now play in the workplace; on the other are those of the older generation with their more prudish sexual mores. The really powerful people in business, however, are still men; their attitudes are conservative, and they are the ones who continue to guide the corporations.

One personnel vice president said, "I've seen some code statements that are so filled with legal verbiage that a man would be afraid to speak to a woman in the office without first speaking to a lawyer." That some men don't deal easily with women is undeniable. A woman senior vice president and director of marketing gave me a perfect example of this. A colleague made a pass at her at work. "He approached me and practically said, 'Go to bed with me.' I did a double-take and said, 'What are you talking about?' And when we discussed it and broke it down, he said, 'Look, I just wanted to establish and build a relationship with you, and this was the only way I knew how to communicate comfortably.' And here's the interesting thing," she went on. "Because of the way he had grown up, there was less risk in being turned down sexually than in approaching me professionally and being turned down as a colleague. That would have been more difficult to accept. But the point of all this had nothing to do with sex; it had, rather, to do with his wanting to get to know me as a friend at work, but he had never done that before with a woman, and he had no idea how to go about it."

As Frederic Withington, a vice president at Arthur D. Little management consulting firm in Cambridge, Massachusetts, puts it, "There have always been a lot of romances, but between people at different job levels. Now what we see is a new pattern. The two are equals, or perhaps the woman is the organizational superior. And that's where the fun lies, because nobody knows how to behave with this new pattern, and this makes the relationship a little more confusing. Now there are professional considerations."

The reactions of men could be predicted in the past, but in this new environment, the organization cannot yet predict what women will do, and what men *with* women will do. They sometimes even try to avoid working together because of the fear of attraction. But this is hardly a solution and only leads to more disruption in the running of the tight corporate ship.

## THE UNCHARTED OPPORTUNITIES

Sexual encounters at work occur for several reasons. The most obvious is simply the availability of sexual opportunities. Among young executives there is the natural attraction of people of the same age, most of whom are not married. In addition, under the guise of business, women have access to men they never had before. A woman can walk up to a man in the same business, or at a convention, conference, or seminar, introduce herself, give him her card, and say, "I'd like to talk to you." These are priceless opportunities for starting relationships. No longer do females have to wait to be asked. They can now make the first move, romantic or otherwise.

Men and women who work together also speak the same language. They understand each other's needs and problems, and this empathy can help lead to closeness and possibly romance. Dr. Carl Eisdorfer, a psychiatrist and president of Mount Sinai Medical Center, observed this natural bonding of people who spend their days together. In a newspaper interview, he said, "People in the same workplace tend to be drawn in the same mold. You are probably more like the people you work with than in many instances you are like the members of your family. The things you read, the things you talk about, the social events you attend in connection with work—all these give the opportunity for warmth and intimacy."

In addition, an advertising vice president pointed out that people are devoting more time to their jobs, and the more time you give to work, the less time you have to seek outside social contacts, so the corporation becomes the natural place to meet people of the opposite sex. This is leading to a new *kind* of romance. The separation between home and office, between a man's and a woman's life, is diminishing. Love and sex and work are often intermingled. It is only conjecture, but the new office romances may, in the end, make marriage stronger and halt the high divorce rate. As people work together and experience the problems of the office, as they understand each other's anxieties and the demands their jobs place on them, marriage may well become more of a shared experience than the unequal relationship it has been.

The growing trend for people to become involved with their

co-workers not only can be seen around most offices, it can be instantly documented in any newspaper. One used to read wedding announcements and note what it was that the fathers of the brides and grooms did. Then suddenly one noticed that the mothers of the brides and grooms also held important jobs. Now not only do the bride and groom generally work, but often they work in the same place. A cursory reading of the *New York Times* wedding announcement pages recently turned up the following:

- Dr. Nancy Goodman and Dr. Peter Torpey, research physicists with Xerox Corporation in Rochester, were married.
- Joan Snyder, an account executive with Herzfeld & Stern, investment bankers, married Richard Lewisohn III, a partner in charge of the corporate finance department in the same firm.
- Sandra Norris is with the investment groups at Prudential-Bache Securities, where her new husband is an assistant vice president.
- Amanda Brown was engaged to Burton Megargel. She deals in fixed income securities for Kuhn Loeb, where he is a vice president.
- Nancy Lin Rose, a doctoral candidate in economics at MIT, married James Michael Poterba, an assistant professor of economics at the same college.
- Susan Helm Lasley married Steven S. Price. Mrs. Price is a brand manager and her husband a senior brand manager for Procter & Gamble in Cinncinati.

One sees the pattern. Love among co-workers seems to be blossoming. However, in no way does familiarity always end in sexual attraction. As Karen Brethower, a psychologist, management consultant, and former vice president for human resource development at Chase Manhattan Bank in New York, said, "It can go in either direction. I think an analogue is the coed dorms. When you see people going around with their stubbly beards, or their hair like a rat's nest, it's not the same as being picked up at eight o'clock to go out to dinner. You see them being tense, angry, in an unguarded position as opposed to being in a courting kind of mode. A lot of the glamour goes out of the opposite sex." She thinks the same thing is true of being together ten hours a day, five days a week at work. "You can't maintain a mask for that length of time, so you see who people really are."

Her comment strengthens the feeling that marriages of the future may have a better chance of enduring, simply because people will know each other better and in a variety of ways before they marry. This is more than mere dating could ever have made possible.

## HOW BIG A PROBLEM?

It is obvious that affairs between male and female executives present a very debilitating quandary for business. We have had so little experience in this area of men and women dealing with each other that we don't know how to approach it.

But as men and women interact more frequently with each other in professional roles, this area will become like other aspects of human relationships, where there is a set of options that people can be realistic about. Right now it's difficult because the set of options is unknown. The history of interactions just isn't there.

It would seem, then, that the more information we can gather, the more accurately we can analyze what precisely is taking place, what is rumor and what is fact. The faster we can build that base of experience, the sooner the intelligent handling of the various options will become second nature to us. Here are some signs of the ferment that has begun:

• In Boston in the spring of 1973, there existed a newspaper called *The Real Paper*. It was flourishing, and relations among the staff members had never seemed closer. But suddenly they became too close. According to a report in *Life and Death on the Corporate Battlefield* by Paul Solman and Thomas Friedman, published in 1982, the associate publisher's wife, who saw the staff frequently, moved in with his close friend, who happened to be the publisher of the paper. People were stunned; the staff was in complete turmoil; people took sides; colleagues became enemies.

Things got nasty when the associate publisher "stole," or took back, his dog from the publisher's house, and it was rumored he would destroy it rather than see it in the arms of his wife and her lover. No one could be fired because they were equal shareholders, and very soon the entire company was sold; in 1981 it collapsed completely. One of the several theories for its demise concerned the chaos caused by the romantic triangle.

• Recently, a vice president of a major corporation told me it was widely rumored that one of the other vice presidents who was on the Board of Directors often flew his girl friend across the country on corporate planes, and was instrumental in convincing management not to sell a subsidiary because his lover was an executive there and he wanted to continue his close corporate and personal friendship.

• On another continent, fifty-one-year-old Bob Aldworth, an innovative executive who tripled the profits of Barclays National Bank of South Africa in only six years, was suddenly fired.

Aldworth, the youngest chief executive in the bank's history, hired Sandra Van Der Merwe as a $2,000-a-day consultant. Van Der Merwe, thirty-six, had excellent credentials. She was the first woman to hold a chair at Witwatersrand University's business school and was the author of four books on marketing strategy. Under her guidance, a number of lucrative new ventures were started. According to a *Newsweek* report, just eighteen months after her arrival, the bank's profits had climbed 18 percent. She was so successful that the bank invested $1.4 million in a new management-consulting venture she organized.

Then, for some reason—perhaps jealousy, or perhaps because of the couple's indiscretions—bank officers began to suspect that Aldworth and Van Der Merwe were more than just business colleagues. When questioned, Aldworth told the truth and admitted he had a "close personal relationship" with the banker. He asked the Board of Directors to believe that "my personal life has not affected my business judgment."

One of the main problems was that both were married to other people, and a romantic affair between two married bank executives could not be tolerated. Commenting on the morality of the situation, the *Rand Daily Mail* wrote: "If strict marital propriety were a necessary condition for a top job in business there would no doubt be a regular number of empty boardroom seats." Nevertheless, Aldworth was forced into premature retirement. This became a boardroom scandal mainly because of the action the bank took.

• A Cleveland, Ohio, judge named Ann Aldrich swore in an affidavit that her district's chief judge, Frank Battisti, had been sending bankruptcy cases to the same law firm where his nephew was a first-year associate, which earned the young man a $40,000 bonus. The accusation was firmly denied by Shimon Kaplan, a partner in that law firm, who happened to be Judge Aldrich's former lover. According to Kaplan, Judge Aldrich was deeply hurt when he refused to marry her and she was simply trying to get even. Once more, careers, reputations, business, and ethical standards were shaken because of a liaison.

The implication is always that some kind of collusion might take place; that people are not spending time working as they should; that some are receiving special favors; that those people at the top are out of control; that something might happen to diminish the value of the corporation; that emotional, rather than business, decisions are being made; that such a person cannot be trusted with important responsibility.

## HOW MUCH SEX IS THERE AND WHAT DOES IT ALL MEAN?

In 1982, Mortimer Feinberg, chairman of BFS Psychological Associates, a New York consulting firm, and Aaron Levenstein, formerly a professor of management at Baruch College, surveyed 112 executives. When asked if they had encountered the problem of on-the-job romance in their own business experience, 82 percent said they had. When asked if their company was adversely affected, a large proportion said it had been. Thirty percent said their company was hurt because of charges of favoritism, 40 percent had been affected by scandal-mongering, another 40 percent had been affected by problems of morale, and 20 percent said other factors had caused damage.

In a more far-ranging study completed in 1977, called "Coping With Cupid," Professor Robert E. Quinn, executive director of the Institute for Government and Policy Studies, State University of New York, Albany, queried business travelers at the Albany and LaGuardia airports. Of the 211 responses, 130, or 62 percent, said they knew of at least one office romance. The nature of the involvements also varied. Professor Quinn characterized them as The Fling, an exciting relationship, which both members of the romantic duo realized would be temporary; True Love, a very sincere relationship that usually involved unmarried people and tended to end in marriage; and, last, The Utilitarian Relationship,

19

in which the man is seeking excitement and sexual experience while the woman appears to be after organizational rewards. There were both positive and negative behavior changes among the couples and others in the companies as a result of these romances. (Details of this part of the study will be described in chapter 2.)

In some cases, notes Professor Quinn, the romance will have little organizational consequence and little effect on the corporation, especially if there are no costs. But in other cases which influence identity, communication, and power, the negative effects of the romance increase and coping strategies can become extreme. Professor Quinn came to the conclusion that the negative results of the romances he studied far outweighed the positive results and that the negative costs to the individual's career and to the corporation were higher.

What then is the significance of this new social phenomenon of sex among executives? According to Princeton sociologist Dr. Charles F. Westoff, it is important in terms of the increasing obfuscation of social roles: "In theory, corporate life is supposed to be distinct from family life. The norm of big business is rationality; it functions best when personal relations and emotions are kept to a minimum. Personal relationships are anathema to the business ethos. They confuse things," he explains, "that shouldn't be mixed up. Now, however, women are increasingly present on equal terms, and situations develop where women in positions of authority can use sex to manipulate men. It may also damage existing marriage relationships," he points out. "The situation has, in addition, created a new kind of career-minded, single woman who, like many a man, wants no more than an affair." Theory and practice have obviously split.

When one thinks of the whole bag of problems resulting from corporate romance, it sounds as though anything resembling romance in the corporation should be banned.

But the reason romances are so disruptive is not that they exist at all—for almost anything in business can cause disruption—but that they are badly handled by both the corporation and the individual. A combination of mismanagement and archaic rules is causing more turmoil in the corporate system than any vital, profitable business could possibly absorb and stay healthy. It is therefore essential, from both the individual and the corporate point of view, to document this sexual element in the changing corporate culture, to examine the new corporation, where power, sex, and paranoia intermingle. Because whether they like it or not, whether it is good for business or bad, corporate romance is as inevitable as earthquakes in California, and it must be explored and understood so that this often unpredictable social force can be properly channeled.

# Chapter 2

# THE UNWRITTEN RULES

$\mathcal{O}$bserving the imminent swarming of women into corporate life, anthropologist Margaret Mead wrote an article for *Redbook* magazine in 1978 in which she urged society to establish taboos against male-female fraternization in the workplace. Her motive was to prevent the harassment of women. She compared such taboos to those operating within families where incest is not allowed. Her warning was clearly and unequivocally stated: "You don't make passes at, or sleep with, the people you work with." (It is interesting to note that Dr. Mead did not follow her own advice. According to her daughter, Mary Catherine Bateson, in her autobiography, *With a Daughter's Eye,* published in 1984, Dr. Mead had a sexual relationship with her teacher, Ruth Benedict, before, during, and after her marriage to Gregory Bateson.)

Even for the less sexually adventurous, Dr. Mead's Victorian-sounding stricture seems an impractical rule. People spend one third or more of their lives at work: their co-workers are the men and women they will be attracted to, will get to know, and know well, and it would be an absurdity to declare all these relationships out-of-bounds. Furthermore, it would be as unworkable as the rules of Prohibition were in preventing drinking. Basic urges and needs cannot be snuffed out by passing a law.

What, really, is a corporation? Is it like Mead's families, which must observe certain taboos, but which presumably also would be governed by the rules of brotherly and sisterly love? I spoke to a sample of executives who tried to characterize those organizations in which they spend most of their lives.

- "A small company like ours is more of a small town. You've got your Peyton Places, where there's cattiness, playing around, all the rest. Our company is an extreme condensation of that."
- "A corporation is a complicated group of groups."
- "It's like the army, with a chain of command, superiors, orders to follow, with the possibility of punishment for those who fail to obey. And the people at the top are just as inaccessible."
- "I don't think it's like family or military. It's not as rigid as the military. You don't salute the boss. The hierarchy is still there, and you have friendly relationships with the people you work with. But it's not like family. It's not even like neighbors."

The corporation is like a nation-state with its own culture, language, and leaders, its own laws, its own society of hierarchies, its own influence, importance, punishments, and rewards. And corporations differ markedly from each other, just as countries do.

Dr. Ralph H. Kilmann, professor of business administration and director of the Program in Corporate Culture at the Graduate School of Business, University of Pittsburgh, thinks the corporation can be looked at in many different ways. "In some ways it's like an army in the way it is structured, in other ways it's like a machine, and in still others, like a family. In the negative sense you could compare it to gang warfare, where there are a lot of pressures on people to behave in certain ways regardless of what the formal document says." He suggests you also can describe the corporation as a political battleground where people are vying for power, glory, and control.

Regardless of how one sees the corporation, they all are immersed in what has come to be known as the "corporate culture." There has been a lot written about this enigmatic social reality, though no one is precisely sure what it means. However one characterizes it, it can be said to be the impetus that governs behavior in the organization and that influences how the corporation will react to romance within its halls.

Dr. Kilmann, who is a consultant to a number of corporations, says the culture is the personality of the company, "the invisible force that guides behavior. It is not what the formal policies, rules, procedures, and job descriptions outline." Culture, he believes, is the shared philosophies, ideologies, values, and beliefs. Furthermore, he continues, "It's the unwritten, often unconscious message that fills the gaps between what is formally decreed and what actually takes place." He adds by way of example that culture seems to form in a company rather quickly, depending on a few critical actions by key individuals. "More than anything else," he explains, "people seem to remember an important incident, like the time that So-and-So got reprimanded for doing a good job just because she was not asked to do it beforehand, and So-and-So got fired because he disagreed with the boss in public, though he was clearly right. These incidents become the folklore that people remember, and indicate what the corporation really wants, or what really counts in order to get ahead—the unwritten rules of the game." People either learn those rules or they get burned.

These nebulous, unconscious norms of behavior, this mysterious culture that each organization has, filter down from the top. If the president or chief executive officer sets the tone of the company, why doesn't it change from time to time as each new person leads in his own style? Simply because that CEO will be chosen, in part, precisely for a style which blends with the corporate culture. Thus, change doesn't happen easily. But it happens.

For example, Albert, the manager of product planning for a large east-coast organization, told me: "The cultural rule when I came to the company was that divorces were really bad. When I got divorced, my boss, who had a very bad marriage, said, 'Are you sure you really want to do this? You're going to ruin your career.'

" 'Hey look,' I said. 'My marriage is going nowhere. I'd rather be single.' "

After the divorce, people began to open up. "One guy told me about how he left his wife, he wanted to marry this other gal, but because of corporate pressure from a higher-level position, he went back to his wife, and has been unhappy ever since. But he did it to save his career. I heard this again and again. It was the corporate culture."

Then something unexpected happened: the corporate president himself got divorced. And the domino effect took over. "Suddenly, in the next level under him," said Albert, "a guy who had confessed to me many times how miserable he was—he had married someone he got pregnant in high school—*he* got divorced." And various others followed suit. These examples of sudden changes in the company's attitude, its unwritten norms—because something has altered top management's views—are happening more often.

In another instance, the tone at a large bank was reversed when the chairman married the woman who was the head of Personnel. While they were engaged, she continued to work there, giving the organization an atmosphere of relaxed sexual freedom. If the chairman could do it, it meant fraternization was allowed. She left after they married.

I asked a Midwestern banker what she would do if she fell in love with a co-worker and the company had a rule against such fraternization. Would she go to her supervisor and discuss the implications? She replied, "I can't imagine that happening. I don't think that any company could dictate your personal life."

A similar naiveté was expressed by a counselor in San Francisco. It merely illustrates the wide degree of difference among the rules, stated or unwritten, in different companies all over the country and abroad. While some employees are treated as though they were vassals in a medieval fiefdom, or economic slaves in a company town where the corporation owns you, your house, and your life, others live and work in bliss, assuming that the corporation could never interfere in anything private.

At one time, corporate rules covered everything from marriage to nepotism to fraternization to dress codes to divorce. Now, because of the discrimination and sexual harassment laws, little but nepotism guidelines and, in some cases, dress codes remain among the written rules. However, in many companies the unwritten pressures are as intimidating as any code could be.

It's difficult to make generalizations on such a shadowy subject as unexpressed strictures, but it seems that older corporations are often the more traditional ones, and the new corporations, like the high-tech companies in "Silicon Valley," the area stretching from Palo Alto to San Jose, California, for example, are apt to be far more liberal, since they employ younger people with more relaxed views of corporate life.

Significant differences exist between large and small companies. In striving for efficiency, the larger corporations have become very bureaucratic and are more likely to have a number of burdensome restrictions, whether written or understood. Small organizations can be looser. They are the ones, for example, that often allow husbands and wives to work together. And in "mom-and-pop" companies there are all sorts of relatives working with each other.

An additional factor in forming rules is where the company is located. There are cultural forces in Atlanta, Georgia, that are not present in Freeport, Maine, or Los Angeles, California. Just as society in general varies from conservative to liberal enclaves, so do the companies that exist in those places vary in their expectations of employee behavior and their standards of morality. A vice president from New York pointed out that when she is in her home office, "Two executives meet, stand a certain distance apart, and shake hands in a pro forma kind of way. You can see square edges around it all. But when I'm out in our California office, it's much more likely to be a hug, even between two men. There is no sexual connotation."

Obviously, the type of industry can make a difference. An employee of an old engineering company described that firm as being "very moral and uptight about personal things like an office romance. They would make things so uncomfortable, you'd leave. But you'd be afraid to do it. It's like the Mother Church." The problem, however, would be totally irrelevant in something like the entertainment industry where stories are rampant about how this or that starlet was "discovered" after having an affair with an industry chief. People couldn't care less. Or, as often happens in a place like a big consulting firm where women travel all over the country and are away for extended periods of time, one expects to hear of many love affairs with clients, some of which become serious and turn into marriage. This happens, as well, in any of the other creative businesses like advertising or publishing where strong value is placed on the individual and his or her needs and eccentricities.

One of the unwritten rules one frequently finds in large corporations (which is nothing but a stereotype masquerading as a rule) is, according to Professor Kilmann, the enduring pressure to treat women as second-class citizens. Even if the law talks of equality, the culture, which was rooted ten, twenty, or fifty years ago, still speaks very poorly of women. Kilmann says: "Some of the norms are such that if you are male and you want to make it up the hierarchy, then you aren't fair to women. You are supposed to put them down. You're supposed to laugh at them just like the other people do.

"And if a male wanted to take an enlightened stand and say, 'Look, this is the twentieth century,' that person would be considered a deviant and a maverick. They are talking this way today in the large corporations."

Professor Jerome Katz of the University of Pennsylvania's

Wharton School also commented on the large corporation's unwritten rules concerning the treatment of women when an office affair takes place. "In my experience," says Professor Katz, "it has been common for companies to ask the woman to leave when they hear of an affair, and there are a lot of reasons for that. Part of it is the institutional sexism in most business," he went on, "and part of it is the anomaly in the labor market. Women come in with less seniority, so you could also say it's the most junior person who is asked to leave, and that would tend to be a woman."

But again, companies vary. In some, they are beginning to ask the man to leave on the grounds that he was the supervisor: he had more responsibility; he should have known; he should have used better judgment.

The most frequent no-no's among the galaxy of unwritten rules are: you cannot marry someone who works for the corporation and remain; you can marry but have to transfer to a different part of the corporation; you cannot have any relationship, an affair or marriage, with anyone you report to, or anyone in direct reporting line to you; you cannot work for the corporation and be married to anyone in personnel (privy to all the salary and confidential records); you also cannot be married to anyone in finance, or anyone in the computer department (they have all the records, too); if you are married, you are forbidden to have any affairs at all in any department with anyone because that is adultery and cannot be allowed; if you are single and have an affair, your chances of promotion may drop drastically; and no family member may work for a competing company.

If this confusion is not enough to daunt any new employee, or even an old hand, there are norms within norms. In some corporations there are global rules and those that may exist just in certain areas. There might be rules in Sales that you don't have in Accounting. A norm in one division of a particular corporation may be that employees don't have to be there at any set time. But the same flexibility of schedule in other departments may not exist.

The same thing might apply to attitudes toward office romance.

For all these reasons, people from the lower track to the top executives are concerned about whether they have read the company signs correctly, and worry deeply about having a romance, wondering whether in some unspoken way an invisible value system is up there passing judgment on them. They wonder too about how much of their personal life to give up for their corporation and their career. It is so easy to guess wrong. Take the case of a woman, a first-level executive, who fell in love with her boss's manager. She had never been married, and he was divorced. They began to date but did not tell the corporation. The man in the middle, who was her supervisor and her lover's subordinate, knew and felt squeezed about giving accurate performance data on her to his manager.

Finally, her supervisor went a couple of levels over the manager to complain. He felt that the affair had hurt their job performances. The woman then was shifted laterally to another department and the man was demoted. They essentially took his stripes away, both to punish him and to set an example. They said, "For someone who has been in the organization a long time and who had management responsibilities, you should have exhibited better judgment. You should have come to us and said, 'Look, we're involved and we need to avoid conflict of interest.' Had you asked to be moved, we certainly would have been sympathetic and done that." In this case, careers were hurt because neither member of the couple had been sensitive to the culture of their company.

The manner in which the company culture is administered is extremely subtle, and it makes having a romance risky. A woman executive who worked for a large pharmaceutical corporation described an affair she had with another executive who was at a slightly lower level. Eventually their relationship broke up. It was only after it was over that she started getting feedback. "I learned that managers at higher levels viewed me as limited because of my relationship with this guy. Their feeling was, 'Her career is over; she's relating to this guy who's at a lower level. We can't promote her any further because that would ruin their relationship.' They start making decisions for you."

## THE DANGERS OF CORPORATE ROMANCE

When confusion or mismanagement reigns because norms and rules to govern new situations are not thought out, disruption in the office can take a variety of forms, some of which researchers have begun to document, and employers to moan over.

Professor Robert Quinn's previously mentioned study of office romance, which was not limited to executives and which was composed of third-party reports, is nevertheless the most complete look at the dangers of such liaisons and how they effect behavior. Sometimes mismanaged, and often *un*managed, such alliances are causing a lot of problems as well as producing some positive results. But in general, business has suffered.

Professor Quinn examined behavior deviations in couples who were reported to have had romances. The impact of their affairs was noticeable.

- The lovers lost the respect of group members in 35 percent of the cases studied. She became preoccupied in 36 percent, and he in 27 percent of the reports. A quarter of them covered the mistakes of their paramours, began to arrive late and leave early, and did less work. He missed meetings in 15 percent of the situations. They became incompetent and made costly errors in 10 percent of the examples. However, the quality of their work dropped in only 16 percent of the cases reported.
- Where power was concerned, males showed favoritism to females in as many as 72 percent of the cases, and females showed it to males in 61 percent. In a third of the situations, he told her things she normally wouldn't

know, and in a quarter of them, he ignored complaints and promoted her. He gave her more power and became inaccessible to others in about 17 percent of the romances.

· She assumed more power in the organization in 22 percent of the cases, isolated the male from other members in 18 percent, flaunted her new power in 14 percent, and gave the male more power in 7 percent of the affairs.

In these examples, the female and the male of the romantic pair reacted much the same way, with a similar percentage of each causing problems. The exceptions were that the women became preoccupied in 10 percent more of the cases than the men, and that the men showed favoritism in 10 percent more of the cases than the women. This is not surprising, since men are more apt to be in power positions.

It appears, then, that complications are rampant in a quarter to a third of most office romances except for the frequency of favoritism, which was the overwhelming troublemaker in two thirds of the reported romances. But there are good consequences of office romance in Professor Quinn's study as well.

Love improved office life in certain instances. In a quarter of the affairs, the men and women were easier to get along with, they were more productive in 16 percent, and changed for the better in 15 percent.

Furthermore, the study also examined the reactions of the lovers' subordinates and colleagues. Interestingly, most of the male's and female's subordinates and colleagues tolerated the relationship but did not approve of it: about two thirds of the subordinates tolerated an affair, but only 24 percent of the male's, and even fewer, 13 percent, of the female's, approved. Among the lovers' colleagues, while as many as 60 percent were willing to tolerate the romance, only 29 percent of the male's, and even fewer, or 19 percent, of the female's, approved. Though disapproving, they apparently did not want to see their colleagues fired.

The study went further and asked about how the subordinates and colleagues coped with the presence of an office affair. About half the couples' colleagues advised them about the relationship, as did a third of their subordinates. While a quarter of the male's colleagues complained to a superior, even more, or one third, of the woman's complained. In a little more than 15 percent of the sample, the couple's subordinates tried to undermine them. In one instance, for example, they leaked damaging information about the work of their boss to a regulatory agency. There was a bit of blackmail as well. When a manager began to reprimand a subordinate for inadequate work, the fellow interrupted and threatened to tell the man's wife about the manager's romantic escapade.

In evaluating the impact of romance, Professor Quinn found that in only a minority of the cases did everyone seem to benefit from the romance with better teamwork and improved productivity. The negative impact far outweighed the positive effects. There was a lot of gossip in most of the cases (70 percent), while in almost a third there were complaints, hostilities, distorted communications, threatened reputations, redistributed work because of someone's absence or inefficiency, the client's awareness of what was going on, and lowered morale.

Women were more disapproving of affairs than were men (perhaps feeling greater jealousy), but surprisingly, workers managed to do their jobs more effectively than would be expected. Productivity dropped in 18 percent of the cases and decision making was slowed in 15 percent, figures that are still unacceptable in any profit-minded company.

The reason morale and productivity are often affected by romance in a corporation, as Professor Quinn observed, is that in many cases it is the male supervisor and his female subordinate who have the affair. What happens then, says management consultant Kaleel Jamison, is that the female manager loses both authority and credibility since those who report to her believe she is being influenced by her lover. She is seen as the man's hand-maiden.

"People no longer trust her to maintain their confidences," says Jamison, "and she no longer gets the information she needs to function effectively. In addition, those in positions below her feel the normal channels for advancement have been blocked, since she is not likely to move up. Thus there is less incentive for these employees to perform at peak levels and seek recognition and promotion."

Employees recoil from any arrangement that looks exclusive, and which then automatically becomes a threat to them. One of the few weapons they have to counteract not being included is gossip. This may be why Professor Quinn noted such a large amount of gossip in the cases he studied. As consultant Arleen LaBella points out, "In our society information is power. And one of the ways you can feel powerful is to have information other people don't have. Gossip, though I don't advocate it, is a way of letting others know that you are, at least in this one sense, impor-tant because you are one of the 'in' people. You know some-thing."

To get beyond the statistics and look at actual behavior and how it affects the individual and the corporation, I spoke with the president of a small Pennsylvania company who told me about his male plant manager who had an affair with a female manager. Both were married. Someone wrote an anonymous letter to the male manager's wife telling her about the affair. Both marriages broke up, and the two lovers moved into an apartment together. The man's performance dropped to 50 percent of normal.

The president did not concern himself with the morality of the situation. "Who are we to judge their morals?" he asked. But what did concern him was performance. He asked his lawyers if he could fire the man. He was advised to prove that the manager's performance had been below par. "I decided not to try," said the president, who showed more concern than the usual large corporation would. "The burden would be on the company. I might ruin his career. I decided to go along with it, but I hired a new assistant manager, just in case. We had to beef up our management team at some expense, in order to have continuity in case the manager left."

Economically, the effect of the affair on the corporation was negative. Besides the added expense of taking on backup employees, production fell, they got behind in shipments, and their deliveries were a month late. Their customers became angry. They had a bad third quarter and lost several hundred thousand dollars. However, at this point, the manager is so grateful for having been given a second chance, the president says he is working at 125 percent of his capability to make up for the damage. In this case, the president created his own company culture, one in which the employee was given enough time to turn around—to everyone's eventual advantage.

## THE CASE OF GINA AND IBM

The confusion about what the cultural norms are, how to manage them even when they are known, and the horrendous mistakes that corporation supervisors are making is no more dramatically shown than in the case of Virginia "Gina" Rulon-Miller. According to the Appeals Court brief prepared by Gina's lawyers, McGuinn, Hillsman & Palefsky of San Francisco, Gina went to work for IBM in 1967 as a nineteen-year-old receptionist in the Philadelphia data center. It was her first real job, and her salary was only $400 a month. At IBM, new employees are always told that career opportunities are available for them as long as they perform satisfactorily and accept new challenges. Gina began to think in these terms and realized she'd get farther if she had a college degree.

She worked all day and went to classes at a university until nine at night. After three years she got her degree, and at the same time kept racking up awards at work. Her first promotion came the year she started work, when she moved from receptionist to equipment scheduler. A year later she got her first merit award as Employee-of-the-Month. After graduating in 1970, she was promoted to systems engineer and transferred to Atlanta, Georgia.

She spent fifteen months as a data processor in Atlanta and then won a job in marketing in the Office Products Division, where she was assured she could have a very exciting career. She was sent to San Francisco and worked as a marketing support representative for two years, training people to use newly purchased equipment.

In 1973 she was promoted again and worked as a liaison person between the drawing board and the marketplace during the development of new equipment. She worked in planning for two years, moving with the job to Texas and Kentucky. She was nominated for another award and urged to go back into sales and someday become a marketing manager. She liked the idea of rising in the management ranks, enrolled at the IBM sales school in Dallas, graduated a class officer, and was assigned to San Francisco. Her career goal was a position in office products division management.

According to IBM policy, she was assigned a performance plan which mapped out the company's annual expectations and later graded her performance. She consistently received the highest ratings and was a member of the One Hundred Percent Club, which means she exceeded the company's expectations of her. Continuously excelling at whatever she did, she received a series of congratulatory letters from her superiors and was promoted to marketing representative. She also won several awards for outselling everyone in her branch during a given month, other awards for the best quota attained in the branch, and still more awards for the best sales quota in the region.

By 1978, she was doing a remarkable job by fulfilling her annual sales quota by the fifth month of the year. This brought her yet another regional award and a special citation for the branch's largest sale—ironically to San Francisco's largest law firm, which would represent IBM in the suit Gina was later to bring against her employer.

Gina's third year in sales culminated with the Golden Circle Award, a coveted company prize which usually went to those who'd been selling for five to ten years. At this point, her branch manager nominated her for the accelerated career development program meant for people who showed the potential to assume IBM management positions and to continue to move up. Since Gina's goal had been to become a marketing manager, and she wanted it so badly, she was overwhelmed with excitement when Philip Callahan, her superior, named her marketing manager of his office products branch. It meant a cut in compensation of $30,000 a year, from $60,000 down to $30,000, but it was viewed as a promotion because of the vast opportunities it promised.

Callahan then drew up a plan for her, the kind IBM reserves for select employees, to show his boss, Gary Nelson. He projected that by 1980 she would have a regional or staff assignment. She was at last a manager and her career looked brilliant and unstoppable.

Then events moved quickly. In March 1979, Callahan predicted another promotion for Gina within eighteen to twenty-four months. In April, she met with regional manager Nelson, who praised her past twelve years at IBM and assured her that her career would keep advancing. In May, IBM gave Gina a six-day vacation in Bermuda in recognition of her work, and she received a $4,000 merit raise. One week later, on June 8, she was fired.

What happened to stonewall Gina's rise through the corporate ranks? According to Gina, on June 7, the day before her last day at IBM, Callahan sent for her. Following is her sworn testimony:

I walked into Phil's office and he asked me to sit down and he said: "Are you dating Matt Blum [manager of QYX, an IBM competitor]?"

And I said: "What?" I was kind of surprised he would ask me and I said: "Well, what difference does it make if I am dating Matt Blum? . . ."

And he said, something to the effect: "I think we have a conflict of interest, or the appearance of a conflict of interest here."

And I said: "Well, gee, Phil, you've, you've pointed out to me that there are no problems in the office because I am dating Matt Blum, and I don't really understand why that would have any, you know, pertinency to my job. You said I am doing an okay job. I just got a raise."

And he said: "Well, I think we have a conflict of interest . . ."

He said: "No" and he said: "I'll tell you what." He said: "I will give you a couple of days to a week. Think this whole thing over."

I said: "Think what over?"

And he said: "You either stop dating Matt Blum or I am going to take you out of your management job."

And I was just kind of overwhelmed.

Then Callahan called Nelson, who was in Hawaii, and reported his conversation with Gina. Despite the fact that he had given Gina time to think about it, he changed his mind and called her in the next day, June 8.

Gina entered Callahan's office and found him sitting ominously behind a desk cleared of any paperwork, an unusual scenario for any IBM manager. She further testified:

I walked into Phil's office, and he asked me to shut the door, and he said he was removing me from management effective immediately. And I said: "What?"

37

And he repeated it. And I was taken aback, I was a little startled, and I think I said: "Well, gee, I thought I had a couple of days to a week to think over the situation that we discussed yesterday."

And he said: "I'm making the decision for you."

And I said: "Phil, you've told me that I'm doing a good job. You told me that we are not losing anybody to QYX because I am dating Matt Blum, that we are not losing any equipment to QYX. I just don't understand what bearing dating has to do with my job."

And he said: "We have a conflict of interest . . ."

I said: "Well, what kind of a job would it be?"

And he said: "Well, I don't have it, but it will be non-management. You won't be a manager again."

"Pardon me? . . ."

And I think I was getting very upset [because] I didn't think that he was following what I thought IBM really did believe in. And he just said: "You know, you are removed from management effective immediately."

And I said: "I think you are dismissing me."

And he said: "If you feel that way, give me your I.D. card and your key to the office. I want you to leave the premises immediately."

And I was just about to burst into tears, and I didn't cry at work, so I basically fled his office.

I felt he dismissed me.

In IBM's version of what took place, Callahan met with Gina on June 7 and asked about her relationship with Blum. Gina responded, "Are you asking me to give up Matt Blum or give up my management job?" Callahan told her, "I need to know about what's going on, if there is in fact a relationship between you and Matt Blum that could be construed as a conflict of interest." Gina then told him, according to Callahan, that her relationship with

Blum was "none of your nor IBM's business," and that he was on "shaky legal grounds." He said he would be back to her shortly. Callahan then tentatively concluded that he had no choice but to reassign Gina. He testified that he then consulted with Nelson, who instructed him to tell Gina that she was being removed from her marketing manager position.

Gina met a second time with Callahan on June 8 and reiterated that her relationship was not IBM's business. Callahan then advised her that she was removed from IBM management in the branch effective immediately and would be assigned to IBM's regional staff in a holding position, with no loss in pay and no loss of job level, and that IBM would find her a job in another division.

In response to her question "Are you firing me?", according to IBM's version of what transpired, Callahan said, "Absolutely not." Callahan testified:

"She said: Well, if that is the case, I prefer to resign from IBM. This isn't the company that I joined twelve years ago. You are not the manager I thought you were. I prefer not to work here."

Gina's lawyers claimed IBM had been guilty of an actual or "constructive discharge." In a constructive discharge, the person is not actually fired, but the alternatives are made so unsatisfactory that he or she is left little choice but to leave. When the case went to court, the jury agreed that one or the other had taken place, and Gina won.

IBM's actions, according to Gina's version, read like the script of a second-rate television movie, melodramatic and unbelievable. Gina had met Blum three years earlier when she became a salesperson in San Francisco. He was an account manager for IBM, and everyone knew they had begun to date. A year later Blum left IBM to work with QYX, an IBM competitor founded by Exxon. They transferred him to Philadelphia, and Gina didn't see him for an entire year, until he was transferred back to San Francisco. They began to date again. No one ever complained or suggested this was a problem, and it certainly was not an obstacle to Gina's awards or promotions.

Gina told the jury that Callahan never mentioned to her that seeing Blum created a conflict of interest. When he confirmed her appointment to management, Gina testified, he had said in passing, "I heard the other day you are dating Matt Blum," and she said, "Oh." And he said, "I don't have any problem with that. You're my number-one pick. I just want to assure you that you are my selection." Regional manager Gary Nelson also knew of the relationship.

What had caused IBM to treat Gina the way they did, to halt the career of an obviously star employee? What were they really afraid of, and what were the details of Gina's relationship that upset them? According to IBM's brief written by their lawyers, Pillsbury, Madison & Sutro of San Francisco, Gina was removed from her position as marketing manager with an offer to reassign her to another division at the same salary "because she was involved in an intimate personal relationship which IBM viewed as creating a 'conflict of interest' between plaintiff's job and her personal life. . . . At the time plaintiff was engaged in a serious romance . . . with the district operations manager of a rival company in direct competition" with IBM. She would be offered a nonmanagement job, but no one knew what it would be.

It was true that Gina dated Blum, but she was not the only IBM employee who had social relationships with him. After leaving IBM and joining the competing firm, Blum was invited to play third base on the IBM baseball team. The games were well attended by IBM salespeople, the pitcher reported directly to regional manager Nelson, and, said Gina's lawyer, "no one ever complained that the infield contained a conflict of interest."

After the games, Blum and his IBM teammates went drinking at a bar not far from the playing field. Blum continued to be part of the IBM crowd, and once, after a wedding of an IBM salesperson, Blum invited Gina, her brother Todd, who also worked for

IBM, and ten or fifteen others to his home. The group included several IBM employees and two IBM marketing managers. They all ended up in a hot tub drinking champagne. No one seemed concerned.

But there were problems. Apparently Callahan's branch was in trouble. His marketing reps were not obtaining their quotas, there was a high turnover, and a number of them were leaving to go with competitors. Office products chief Terry Notari warned Nelson and other regional managers that it was extremely important to hold on to high achievers like Gina. There was considerable fear that QYX and Matt Blum would steal IBM's best people away.

Instead of ignoring Gina's private life as long as she was doing a superb job, or discussing the situation with her intelligently, Callahan bungled his own job badly when he called Gina to his office and took her out of management.

Why had he done it? Perhaps because following her interview with her boss, Gina had gone to a going-away party for a cousin at a restaurant. With her were her brother, her cousin, his wife, two family friends, and Matt Blum. By coincidence Ray Green, Nelson's manager of regional marketing, was also dining at the same restaurant. According to testimony at the trial, Green spotted her, called Nelson in Hawaii, and reported that he had seen Gina, Blum, and "what he thought were other QYX people" at an apparent celebration. Nelson then passed on this report to Callahan.

In their brief, IBM contends that Gina broke the Business Conduct Guidelines which state that "IBM employees and members of their immediate families should not have an investment or other financial interest in a competitor that could create a divided loyalty or the appearance of one" and that they cannot serve as an advisor to a competitor.

Their rules also state that "employees must avoid personal conflicts of interest ... free from the influence of personal consider-

ations or relationships when dealing for IBM with others. . . ."
It is hard to believe that anyone as devoted to her career as Gina
was an advisor to a competitor.

Also, at one point, two of Gina's co-workers, Wayne Fyvie and
Mary Hrize, had evidently reported gossip that worried Callahan.
They told him that Gina and Matt were living together, and
Fyvie mentioned that he'd spotted them at a tea dance at the
Hyatt Regency Hotel. Both, however, stated at the trial that they
never thought Gina would be disloyal, they merely worried about
appearances.

Questions that came up during the 1981 trial elicited some
significant answers. They dramatically point up the fact that
business conduct and social conduct are two separate things, and
though at times they may cross, they do not have to, and can be
kept completely distinct. This is one of the new realities which
is so difficult for business to understand, because it remains bur-
dened with musty, outmoded stereotypes. Gina's boss Callahan
was asked: "Does IBM have a policy that requires an employee
to terminate friendships that they have made with fellow employees, if that fellow employee leaves IBM to go to work for a
competitor?"

CALLAHAN: No, they do not.

Regional manager Nelson was asked: "Is it a policy of IBM's
to discourage the appearance of socializing with other competitor
employees?"

NELSON: There is no policy that states what you just said.

Nelson was then asked: "In fact, IBM has no policy whatsoever
regarding individuals' [social] relationships outside of IBM with
competitors or noncompetitors, correct?"

NELSON: If I understand your question correctly, yes.

When Hrize testified at the trial, she was asked: "Is there any question in your mind whatsoever that Gina would ever do something disloyal to IBM?"

HRIZE: No question in my mind.

"That she would not?"

HRIZE: She would not.

Callahan was then asked: "Prior to June 7, was there any evidence of an actual adverse impact on the job performance of any other IBM employee due to Gina's relationship with Matt Blum?"

CALLAHAN: The answer to that question is no.

Callahan was also asked, "Am I correct that as of June 7 you had no direct evidence or suggestion that there was an adverse impact on IBM's reputation because of Gina's relationship with Matt Blum?"

CALLAHAN: That is correct.

Then Nelson was asked if he could explain the company's fears. "Can you identify for me a single employee prior to June 7, 1979, that you know of [who] . . . did not have confidence in Gina Rulon-Miller?"

NELSON: I personally, no.

Gina apparently had not broken any rules, was not disloyal, caused no disruption, was not besmirching IBM's reputation, had not adversely affected anyone's job performance (or lowered her own), had not violated any rules regarding conflict of interest in her personal life (which did not exist), had no more of a business conflict of interest than did many others who had friendships (and presumably affairs) outside the company, was devoted to her own company, and was not planning to throw away all the work she'd put into getting ahead at IBM.

In 1968, IBM chief executive officer Tom Watson wrote an important memo to all managers that was still in effect when Gina was fired. He said some useful things that perhaps can clarify just how to deal with this growing conundrum over what a company can and cannot demand of its employees regarding their private lives. The CEO wrote:

"The line that separates an individual's on-the-job business life from his other life as a private citizen is at times well-defined and at other times indistinct. But the line does exist. . . . I have seen instances where managers took disciplinary measures against employees for actions or conduct that are not rightfully the company's concern. These managers usually justified their decisions by citing their personal code of ethics and morals or by quoting some fragment of company policy that seemed to support their position. . . . What we need, in every case, is balanced judgment which weighs the needs of the business and the rights of the individual. . . .

"We have a concern with an employee's off-the-job behavior only when it reduces his ability to perform regular job assignments, interferes with the job performance of other employees, or if his outside behavior affects the reputation of the company in a major way. When on-the-job performance is acceptable, I can think of few situations in which outside activities could result in disciplinary action or dismissal. Furthermore, the damage must be clear beyond reasonable doubt and not based on hasty decisions about what one person might think is good for the company.

"IBM's first basic belief is respect for the individual, and the essence of this belief is a strict regard for his right to personal privacy. This idea should never be compromised easily or quickly."

Judging from Watson's memo, it seems to me that his opinion would be that Nelson's and Callahan's suddenly hostile treatment of one of their most valued employees went beyond the bounds of fairness, logic, good sense, or good management. By its actions, IBM was saying that it is impossible for a man or woman to have a romantic relationship with anyone else in the field in which he or she works, since most companies in any given field are naturally competitive with each other. Yet these are the people one gets to know—at work, conventions, and meetings. Such companies are saying, "We cannot trust you to manage two separate parts of your life fairly—social and business—when romance is involved." And as they try to abolish the natural friendship, romance, and mating of male and female business associates, the prohibitions get bigger, more complex, more prejudiced, and more impossible to enforce.

After her final meeting with Callahan, Gina left the office in tears. She had taken a $30,000-a-year compensation cut to get into management and suddenly she was out of it forever. She testified that she was hysterical following the meeting, was unable to function for months, not able to get out of bed or look for a job, and spent most of her time crying. She eventually pulled herself together, was hired by another firm, Wang, and is now making more than she was making when she left IBM.

In a speech to the American Bar Association, Gina's lawyer, Cliff Palefsky, said when speaking about prospective clients' states of mind, "You aren't looking across your desk at a broken leg. You are looking at a shattered ego, a person thrust into an identity crisis, a person with a very big face to save." In a situation where a person is fired although she or he has been performing superbly, emotional stress can be very real and severe. Palefsky acknowledged that he had two clients who actually attempted suicide.

In the same speech, when demonstrating a potential argument to a jury, Palefsky continued, "Corporations have no conscience, they have accountants. Corporations don't worry about going to heaven when they die. A large corporation can have utter disrespect for the individual, for the human spirit. The corporate mentality can strip human beings of respect and significance." He might well have been talking about IBM and Gina Rulon-Miller.

How much this experience really hurt Gina may be imagined by noting the comments of a woman who works at IBM. She said, "People who work for IBM really love IBM. They *are* IBM. They are IBMers. They internalize the values of that company and believe themselves to be enmeshed in the spirit." To be thrown out would, indeed, be horrible, one of life's worst conceivable traumas.

This whole case might never have come to trial had IBM been willing to pay Gina the severance she felt they owed her for firing her. She would probably never have attempted to correct what she felt was a gross injustice. But they refused to give her a penny, insisting that she had quit. It was for this reason that she sought a lawyer. Then the jury backed her up with a unanimous vote agreeing that she had been fired, and awarded her $300,000 for wrongful discharge and intentional infliction of emotional distress.

Why didn't the jury consider Gina's relationship with Matt Blum a conflict of interest? Palefsky said that, to him, a conflict of interest implies an economic conflict "where she gains if an IBM competitor gains." He said, for example, "If you own stock in a competitor and that company does well, you win. In Gina's situation, if the competitor did well, it would reflect poorly on her, it would negatively affect her job in every way. She was a loyal, hard-working stockholder of IBM.

"They are saying she had personal feelings for the guy. So what? There is no question they were competitors, and she had no motivation to do anything but compete actively against him. The only reason they can suggest a conflict," said Palefsky, "is if they use some ridiculous sexist notion, and assume that since she is a woman, she would automatically sacrifice her life and career because she was in love with this guy." He pointed out that there are friendships everywhere. It's only a conflict when there is economic gain, and "under none of the scenarios would she ever have benefited.

"To make the point," he continued, "it is not unlike two men who used to work together who now compete against each other but remain friends. The only difference is sex, what people do once they close the bedroom door. That's not conflict of interest. That's life. Being drinking buddies," he continued, "probably poses as much of a threat as Gina's relationship."

The problem is the mythic stereotype that women in love will act irrationally and men will not. No one worried about the impropriety or danger to the corporation from Matt Blum's fraternizing with the IBM men, playing baseball and drinking with them. The fact that Gina was a woman allowed her superiors to feel justified in questioning her motives.

It is common in many industries for people to change jobs to get ahead. They invariably end up working for competitors and continue to see old friends. It is ludicrous to think that a relationship which is all right when both are working for the company, say in different departments, will become intolerable for the company if either person goes to a competing company. Is it realistic to expect them to break off the relationship? Should either of them be forced to leave a job in which they may have a strong emotional and professional stake?

Furthermore, consider the many young men and women executives who *marry* others in the same field but who work for competing companies. Don't they have a conflict of interest? When Rebecca Loomis, a senior account executive for CNA Insurance Companies in Houston, married DeWitt Smith, a group manager with the Prudential Insurance Company, also in Houston, was either company concerned? Of course not. For some reason, a marriage to a competitor seems less threatening than an *affair* with the same competitor. An affair makes everyone's behavior more suspect in conservative company eyes than does a marriage, though either situation could produce harmful effects such as stealing employees or exchanging secrets.

But one does not have to have a romance or a marriage to create an atmosphere in which company information could be compromised. One merely has to have lunch in a Silicon Valley restaurant, says *The Wall Street Journal,* to pick up the best-guarded secrets being discussed across the cheese and bean-sprout sandwiches. There is simply no foolproof guarantee that any company can keep fences around its star executives, plans for new products, or sales campaigns and advertising information, or excise from an individual's mind the intellectual property he has acquired while working. To rise up in alarm over a possible conflict of interest between those who have an intimate relationship and also work for competing companies is to focus unnecessary attention on this one group.

Unhappy with its stinging defeat at the hands of a jury, IBM decided to appeal. They lost once more. In a landmark opinion handed down in 1984, the judges affirmed the verdict of the lower court. Quoting the "Watson Memo," the Appeals Court said, "It is clear that this company policy insures to the employee both the right of privacy and the right to hold a job even though 'off-the-job behavior' might not be approved of by the employee's manager." The judges also said that although IBM had the right to terminate an employee for "conflict of interest," the "record showed that IBM did not interpret this policy to prohibit a romantic relationship." IBM managers all admitted such a rule did not exist and employees did not have to "terminate friendships with fellow employees who leave and join competitors." Furthermore, the court noted that while Gina was successful, her job did not give her access to sensitive information that she could give a competitor.

As the Appeals Court saw it, there was no decline in morale, and Gina's outside activities did not interfere with her work. They felt the "conflict of interest" charge was untrue, and that it was used as a pretext to terminate Gina.

Since the right of privacy is guaranteed by the California state constitution, the question is, said the court, "whether the invasion of [Gina's] privacy rights by her employer . . . constitutes extreme and outrageous conduct." In examining the case, the court noted, "There was a decided element of deception in Callahan acting as if the relationship with Blum was something new." The evidence was clear that he knew of her involvement well before her promotion. Second, "he acted in flagrant disregard of IBM policies prohibiting him from inquiring into [Gina's] 'off-job behavior.' By giving [Gina] 'a few days' to think about the choice between job and lover, he implied that if she gave up Blum she could have her job." He then did not give her the few days or the right to choose.

"So far the conduct is certainly unfair but not atrocious. What brings Callahan's conduct to an actionable level is the way he brought these several elements together in the second meeting with [Gina]. He said, after calling her in, 'I'm making the decision for you.' The implications of his statement were richly ambiguous, meaning she could not act or think for herself, or that he was acting in her best interest, or that she persisted in a romantic involvement inconsistent with her job. When she protested, he fired her.

"The combination of statements and conduct would under any reasoned view tend to humiliate and degrade [Gina]. To be denied a right granted to all other employees for conduct unrelated to her work was to degrade her as a person." The Appeals Court concluded that by removing "any free choice on her part contrary to [Callahan's] earlier assurances also would support a conclusion that his conduct was intended to emphasize that she was powerless to do anything to assert her rights as an IBM employee. *And such powerlessness is one of the most debilitating kinds of human oppression.* [Emphasis added.] The sum of such evidence clearly supports the jury finding of extreme and outrageous conduct." The court then upheld Gina's $100,000 in compensation and $200,000 in punitive damages, totally affirming the jury's verdict.

When IBM finally brought this case before the California

Supreme Court, it refused to hear it, thereby once more affirming the lower court's decision and the Appeal Court's opinion. Lacking IBM's financial or legal resources, one young woman nevertheless had beaten the mighty corporate giant.

## IS THERE A RIGHT TO PRIVACY?

Companies seem to be free to invade the private boundaries and roam the most sacred realms of people's minds, or at least they think they are or ought to be. Are there no federal privacy laws to protect employees against managerial inquisitions on where, when, with whom, and at what they spend their time away from work? According to Palefsky, there is no express right to privacy in the U.S. Constitution. But in the 1960s, when the Supreme Court handed down decisions on birth control, abortion, and cohabitation, it said, in effect, that when you look at rights guaranteed in the First Amendment (freedom of speech), the Fourth Amendment (freedom from unreasonable searches and seizures), and the Fifth Amendment (freedom not to be deprived of life, liberty, or property without due process of law), the penumbra from all those amendments created a right to privacy. Or as U.S. Supreme Court Justice Harry A. Blackmun called it, "certain areas or zones of privacy." The Constitution not only is not specific on this subject, but "more important," says Palefsky, "it only prohibits certain kinds of government activities. It doesn't tell you what a private citizen or a private corporations can or cannot do."

There are at least fifteen states that have provisions in their state constitutions guaranteeing the right to privacy. California, of course, is one of them, and it applies to everyone—individuals, corporations, and the government. In Palefsky's interpretation of this law, it means that a corporation cannot invade an individual's right to privacy without "a compelling business interest." And in Gina's case, that did not exist.

The cost of Gina's corporate romance is easily totaled up: the disruption of a career, with resulting mental anguish; the loss to the corporation of a star employee whose departure probably lowered morale and hurt productivity even further; damage to the company's reputation for caring about its employees; the cost to the corporation of hundreds of thousands of dollars in lawyer's fees; the corporation's loss of the valuable time several of its managers have devoted to the court case and the resulting appeal. Profit? Zero. Nobody wins.

## WILL YOUR CORPORATE CULTURE ALLOW ROMANCE?

Horror stories of this kind are caused by supervisors' shocking mismanagement of corporate romance. However, such tales are only the dark side of the moon. Corporate romance can be happy, exciting, permissible, well managed, an impetus to increased devotion to the job, and a spur to higher productivity. A relationship can be all the things romance is supposed to be. It all depends on what industry, what company, what culture. Here are three examples of corporate romance with happy beginnings, middles, and endings.

An executive in a major New York advertising firm met her husband-to-be, who was in the same firm, when they worked together on an account. "He was several levels above me at that point. Working together we developed a mutual respect and friendship that was a real luxury. Though our relationship didn't begin until after the project ended, it was a very interesting experience getting to know someone well through work before becoming involved romantically."

After they began dating, they saw and talked to each other every day at work. Though he was her ultimate boss in the line of command, she did not report to him directly. Because they had gotten to know each other so well at work, their friendship became very solid, and they knew that it was going to be serious and not a "quick hit."

When they realized how permanent it might be, he informed their mutual superior. They didn't want to work together. Also, "we figured probably the quickest way to become old news is to let everybody know," she said. "People only talk if there is something secretive about it. Then there's a lot of speculation and gossip. This way, we acknowledged it, there was some talk about it for a while, but it subsided and became an accepted thing. I was never aware of any catty or jealous remarks." He was not in a position where he could directly affect her career.

When they announced that they were getting married, they had wondered what would happen, because although there was no written rule against nepotism in their company, there was an implicit feeling that it isn't done. In this case, it didn't affect them. She thinks it was because "if you happen to meet someone when you are both working for the corporation, if you established separate careers, and separate career paths, then met and married, the nepotism rule wouldn't apply. However, if you married someone outside and tried to bring your spouse in, they would discourage it."

He no longer works for the same company, but it has nothing to do with their marriage. He had one of those opportunities one can't refuse and now is in a competing advertising company. While they worked together, she felt they both benefited and their productivity greatly increased.

In another case, a woman senior vice president of one of the largest banks in her state met the man she would marry when they were both officers taking a high-level management-training class. They didn't start dating for several years. He was married at the time, and though she saw him quite a lot, it was all business.

One day about two years after they met, they had coffee together and ended up having dinner. He had just gotten a divorce. They started dating.

Neither reported to the other, but an occasional client would be a customer of both. There were no rules at the bank about fraternization, and many officers married people in the organization. A bank rule against such marriages had disappeared along with similar rulings in the mid-Sixties, when many companies dropped them.

After dating for a year, they were engaged. When I asked her if she had gone to her supervisor to discuss it, she replied in astonishment, "Oh, heavens no, I didn't feel I should. Besides," she laughed, "by that time we were both vice presidents, and I was a division head. Who would I go to?"

But wasn't there any feeling among the other officers that they would get special favors, pull a double weight?

"The bank is large enough so there is no way we could have exerted undue influence on others. There was never any problem," the woman said, "and we weren't flirting during the work day. We were both really busy with our respective jobs. We didn't have coffee together during the day. I think if we had, that might have caused some negative comment. We came into work together, and we left together, and that's about it. We just weren't holding hands all day."

Unlike many, she did not keep her maiden name. She thought it would be too difficult with both of them in the organization. "If we worked with the same client and he knew me by one name and my husband by another, it would be confusing, and I did not want to go through life explaining."

Working in the same place does not put an extra burden on their marriage. "Quite the opposite," she said. "I love our being able to relate to each other's work environment and to all the people we're involved with during the day. We each understand what the other is doing." They are, in fact, a perfect example of the excitement that a corporate romance and the subsequent marriage can create. The closeness they feel, the interest in each other's problems, the ability to understand each other's work, are stimulating and add both to their job and to their marriage.

"We often discuss problems. It's wonderful. We help each other. And there's enough private life aside from business. Actually," she said enthusiastically, "we have something which few married couples have. We drive to work, about an hour each way. In the morning we chat a bit and plan the day's schedule. But on the way home, we have a full hour to exchange news about what we did that day. Then by the time we arrive, we're off the subject of the office.

"My advancement was spectacular after we married," she remembered, "and my husband's work improved because he was a happier person."

The third example involves two young lawyers who were associates in a very conservative New York firm of over 200 lawyers. They met at a firm dinner-dance, dated for a while, and, quite deliberately, agreed not to tell anyone. "We didn't go public until it was very clear we were serious," he said. That was three weeks before they became engaged.

"I wanted to avoid the possibility of hurt feelings and discomfort if the relationship should break up and we both remained at the firm," he said. The two people involved might have a very good understanding, but no one else would.

She agreed. "They wouldn't know how to behave. Any people who've broken up make others feel slightly uncomfortable. They don't know what to say."

Initially it was no problem. The problem came when somebody they both knew had a party. The question was, should they go together, separately, or not at all? "I have no patience with that kind of mucking around," she said. They finally decided just to go and see if anybody cared.

"Actually, there wasn't really much of a stink about it," she said and laughed. They began to tell friends. "It really had a lot less impact than I expected. I was surprised." She said the week before they were engaged, they went skiing together. The firm routinely sends an out-of-town sheet around for all the lawyers to note where they will be if they are away from the office. On this sheet, two lawyers would show up in the same tiny town in Vermont, gone for exactly the same length of time. "I thought, 'Boy, if people didn't know, they'll know now.' " Some noticed and some didn't.

But the reaction in the firm was one of pleasure. "I asked the managing partner in my group if it was all right, because I know some firms do have a policy where they ask some people to leave," he said, "but he told me they were very happy we were getting married, and they wanted both of us to stay very much." They'd had marriages in the firm twice before. It is interesting to note, however, that if a partner (one of the lawyers who own and run the firm) married an associate (a lawyer who merely works for the firm), the associate would be expected to leave, because that associate might be perceived to be treated better than the others.

He put his finger on a crucial difference between law and, say, manufacturing. "A law firm doesn't have the corporate hierarchy," he pointed out, "where you can say there are twenty-one levels in this corporation, or forty-two, and someone who happens to be two levels above you actually exerts a tremendous amount of power over you."

The differences in attitude that various kinds of companies have toward romantic relationships are striking. While large corporations, like those in manufacturing, sales, and marketing, seem more likely to present problems to amorous couples, financial institutions, advertising, and law, which have a looser structure, seem to provide happy endings. In neither kind of place, however, does anybody seem absolutely certain of what the culture says about such matters. There is always a lot of trepidation involved, uncertainty about whether to approach a supervisor, and what he or she will say. In the back of employees' minds are the questions, Are we guilty? Are we doing something wrong? Or is it all okay?

## Chapter 3

# ARCHAIC ATTITUDES

*S*everal fortunate executives I interviewed remarked that they could not imagine the corporation intruding into a person's private life. "It's none of their business" was a frequent response. But other employees are not nearly so lucky.

Though some corporations appear to want to offer their employees an atmosphere free of all personal, restrictive rules, and some, as we have seen, attempt to control personal behavior through subtle, unwritten rules that exert inhibiting pressures, other corporations are stubbornly adhering to strongly spelled-out, outdated rules (sometimes written and sometimes not) which place extreme strictures on the private lives of their executives. While the ideal corporation is trying to be more informed and farsighted in charting its future, some seem to be taking one giant step backward. Such companies try to determine whom their executives will date, fraternize with, live with, or marry. Some even check on who is sending flowers to whom.

A woman named Doris Cooper Baxter got a job as a stewardess for United Airlines in 1967. The airline at the time had a rule that stewardesses could not marry. When Baxter married anyway, she had to leave. Other stewardesses chose to go to great lengths to keep their jobs. They concealed marriages, did not wear their wedding rings, and gave up or hid their children. In many cases it was necessary to keep two phones in their homes. One number was given to business associates and the other was kept for personal relationships. Their husbands were never allowed to answer the business phone. Some women were said to put maiden names on their mailboxes, and there were stories, denied by the airline, that employees were assigned to check newspapers for wedding announcements, and to harass or ground women suspected of secretly marrying or having a baby.

United, whose no-marriage rule was rescinded in 1968, has not been the only company to have such regulations. Unfortunately, today, the atmosphere in some corporations remains as forbidding and restrictive, and the codes are laced with enough prohibitions to turn a normal, healthy person into a paranoiac.

## NO ADULTERY ALLOWED HERE— SLOHODA *v.* UNITED PARCEL SERVICE

Everyone is familiar with United Parcel Service, whose oversized brown trucks deposit wonderful packages at one's door. I always considered United Parcel Service men efficient and pleasant and United Parcel as American as baseball in July. Then one day I heard about Jon Slohoda.

When I talked to him, Jon was thirty-five years old and the father of four children. He had recently been fired from his $50,000-a-year job as a supervisor at UPS in New Jersey, where he had worked successfully for ten years.

In March 1982, Jon filed suit against UPS charging discrimination on the basis of marital status, conspiracy to discriminate to interfere with his employment relationship, and deprivation of his right to privacy as guaranteed by the New Jersey state constitution, among other things. There followed a long legal process which has not yet ended. The chronology reads like this:

1982: Sworn depositions were taken of Jon and several UPS managers.

1983: Motion for summary judgment, in which UPS asked to have the case dismissed for lack of cause. Judge Rumana agreed with the UPS position and dismissed the case.

1984: Slohoda appealed to the Superior Court and won his

appeal, and the case was reinstated in February.

1984: In December, the trial was held before the same Judge Rumana. It lasted one week, during which Jon Slohoda's side was presented to a jury. When it came to UPS's turn to present their version of what transpired to cause them to fire Jon, UPS lawyers presented a motion to dismiss the case, and Judge Rumana dismissed it for a second time. The jury never heard the UPS argument and never was able to make a decision.

1985: Slohoda is appealing again and will try for a different location and a different judge.

According to testimony, the following took place: Jon and his wife, Gail, had been having marital difficulties and had been to a psychologist. Jon began seeing Patti Arnett, a single UPS hourly driver whom he supervised. She was later promoted into management, and no longer reported to him.

Jon left his wife, and he and Patti began to live with each other in January 1981. They kept the relationship secret, telling only one or two of their close friends, coming to work and leaving separately, and keeping to themselves on weekends. In May, Jon told his supervisor, Division Manager Jim Barry, with whom he was friendly, that he was no longer living with his wife, Gail. Jon said, "Basically I told him that I had left my wife in January. He was sympathetic. He mentioned to me he was surprised that I married her in the first place, because she was such a dishrag. Those were his exact words. He would love to do the same thing if he could find an older woman who was rich. And he offered me a raise, asked if I needed a raise, or if there was anything he could do to help me. And I said no to both things."

He did not tell Barry he was living with Patti because he thought "it was none of his business," and he would keep anything secret if he felt Barry's knowing would invade his privacy. He also said he was not aware of any rule or policy against sexual relationships between managerial personnel and employees of the opposite sex.

Then one day Barry, who had learned of the Slohoda-Arnett liaison, called him in and asked him if he was living with Patti. Being an honest fellow, Jon said yes.

Barry was questioned when he gave his deposition:

Q: Did you inform him there was no chance of advancement or a more responsible job because of the situation he was in with Patti?

A: I guess I may have said that when it blows over he has a shot.

Q: Now, at that time didn't you tell Jon that he blew his career for a woman?

A: I may have said something similar to that.

Q: Did you tell him that you were personally angry at him for leaving his wife and kids?

A: Yes, I think I did.

Jon said Barry told him, "One of you will have to resign," and he thought that what Jon was doing was embarrassing to the company.

According to Jon, he was told the company didn't like him to fraternize with anybody at UPS, but part of his job required him to take people out for group functions, business meetings, and parties, and it was common to go out after work and have drinks together. Once you fell in love, however, you broke their unwritten rule about fraternization. This came out afterwards. Jon had never heard of that before.

Although UPS managers alluded to an unwritten rule about fraternization, they did not seem clear about its substance. When questioned, District Personnel Manager William Balzer described the rule as follows:

Q: Can you describe for me the company policy regarding fraternization?

A: We do not want our management people fraternizing with other employees of the company.

Q: What does that mean?

A: Our feeling—our position is that . . . a management person having a personal involvement with another person, I have to say, of the opposite sex at this point. We don't want that.

Q: What are the reasons for not wanting that?

A: One, the people involved lose their objectivity. I think we have the loss of confidentiality on certain items.

Q: Is this regardless of whether or not one of the parties involved supervises another person involved?

A: That's anyone in management.

Q: Regardless of whether they're even in the same building or not?

A: Correct.

Q: Is that policy you just described written anywhere?

A: No.

Division Manager James Barry thought the "policy" was in writing but couldn't say where it could be found. And former District Manager Richard Boland, who was transferred to Minnesota in 1982, described the "policy" or "rule" as being unwritten, but from his "own personal view," it has been in effect since August 1959.

Balzer was questioned further about fraternization:

Q: Are you aware of any management personnel dating one another or fraternizing with one another after hours at bars like Bucky's, [which] is a common place, as I understand?

A: Yes. Male and female supervisors do get together after work.

Q: Does that violate the rule?

A: Not in that context.

Q: When does the rule become violated?

A: When the heart gets involved.

Q: In light of Mr. Hoyt and Mr. Holland [two UPS employees

who married other employees with whom they had had personal relationships]—do you think it's a rule that has been broken before?

A: I have to say yes, based on that.

When he was told either he or Patti would have to go, Jon said he had no intention of resigning, since he felt he had done nothing wrong, and that if they wanted Patti to resign, they should talk to her. He certainly wouldn't make a decision like that for her. He didn't argue with his supervisor. He said, "I could tell right away his direction was already predetermined. It seemed he knew where he was going."

The shocking thing for Jon was that Barry and he were friends. "It wasn't like he was a stranger to me. We had gone out about twice a week and had a couple of drinks and talked, and now, rather than approach me on a social level, or as a friend, or someone who was concerned, he flat-out took the corporate stand. So there was really no reasoning with him."

His supervisor did not call Patti in to speak about her resigning. On June 17, the day after telling Jon one of them would have to leave UPS, Jim Barry called Jon at home at about ten o'clock in the evening and asked if he and Patti could meet him and Bill Balzer the next morning. Jon said he would be glad to and was told to meet them at Smith Field, a park in Parsippany. The four of them sat on a bench.

Balzer was questioned:

Q: Why did you choose that place?
A: It was quiet. It was a warm day. I get tired of sitting in restaurants.
Q: Why would you meet in a restaurant or park instead of at UPS?
A: For privacy.

According to Jon, Bill Balzer began by saying, "Let's start from the back and go forward. Are you two going to get married?" Jon said they didn't know. Then, said Jon, Balzer "made mention that we had to get our guts out of it . . . both sides had to get their guts out of it so we can talk about this serious problem, as he referred to it, intelligently.

"Both Patti and I told him our guts weren't in it. We were more than willing to cooperate." Barry and Balzer told the two that "they frowned on fraternization and when they find out about it they have to act. I believe he said 'act quickly and severely.'

"He asked us if we understood why this type of thing could not be allowed at UPS, and we answered that we did not understand, because we felt it had absolutely no effect on the business and, in fact, it aided us in both being better at our jobs."

The managers then told Jon that it was harmful to the business because "we would start taking too many days off, missing too many days at work. . . . I said to them we have not to this point. There is no reason why we should. And if we did, if that did become a problem, I'd be more than glad to discuss it with them."

Jon said the men next told them it hampered the business because they could not be assigned to the same center at any one time, and Jon pointed out there were enough openings and so much flexibility that they could easily arrange to be in different locations. Jon said they were aware of the antinepotism policy at UPS, and if they got married, one of them would resign. But "at this point, since we did not know what we were going to do as far as getting married or not, that we would not arbitrarily resign because it wouldn't be fair to the one who resigned. . . . Say if Patti or I resign, then two months later our relationship broke up, there is no reason to sacrifice a career on what might happen. . . . We didn't want to cause any trouble. We just wanted to be left alone and maintain our privacy."

Mention was made of other management people who had

cohabited and continued to work for the company. Later, when they married, one would leave the company. Jon said that Bill Balzer commented that his case was different because the other people were "single folks and that me being married made a difference."

"They both admitted they could not detect any deterioration in our job performance. . . . They had no complaints about anything that had happened as far as the job goes. . . . There were no conclusions drawn despite Patti and I both asking for a little guidance as far as what they expected us to do next or how we could cooperate. They just left it up in the air."

In his deposition, Balzer commented, "I would have to say that . . . this was a reflection on UPS. That we had an individual who had left his wife and had a relationship with a supervisor in UPS. And I guess I have to say I felt that this was unacceptable."

"That was all we spoke about," said Jon. "They were just out there trying to do a little head-searching to see where we were coming from. Patti was newer to the company than I, and she was just in utter disbelief that in the 1980s this could be happening. She was flabbergasted by the whole thing."

The next day, a meeting was called with all the management people in the building. A friend, who is no longer with the company, was present at the meeting and told Jon what was discussed. The group was told there was a very serious problem in the district, that Patti and Jon were living together, and "that none of them should talk to Patti or me," Jon said, "if they valued their careers, and that down the road they would get me."

According to Jon, no one had complained about his job performance. He had an impeccable record, and in fact he was doing better than ever because he was so happy. After he started living with Patti, the production rating for his center improved. "I was in a much better frame of mind," he said, "and at the end, I was the number-one operation in the district out of sixteen similar operations."

It was not long after the meeting in the park that Jon noticed that his fellow employees, with whom he normally got along very well, stopped talking to him. From June until August he was given the "silent" treatment.

Q: Do you mean people literally didn't talk to you?
A: Unless they had to. Yes. They were instructed not to.
Q: Who instructed them?
A: Well, I was told Jim Barry did . . .
Q: Didn't you think this was an outrageous kind of thing for Barry to do?
A: I certainly did.
Q: Were you not surprised, having had such good relations, that a whole bunch of men, fit and healthy, would obey such instructions?
A: I was flabbergasted, to say the least.

Jon admitted that he had received similar instructions with respect to several other employees. Jim Barry had told him, for example, "Don't talk to MacDonald," about a year before, because "they were trying to fire him." He said he had obeyed the instruction.

When James Barry was asked about whether he really ordered the silent treatment for Jon, he responded in this way:

Q: Did you ever at any time tell people not to talk to Jon and Patti?
A: Those words?
Q: Yes.
A: I told people to be careful of what they said to Jon and Patti.
Q: Why did you tell them that?
A: I heard from others that Jon was writing a book.
Q: Who had you heard it from?
A: Other managers.
Q: Who?

A: Other managers.
[He then mentioned three names.]

When asked if he had ever warned other managers or supervisors not to talk to other employees, he said he had warned them to be careful of what they said to other employees he felt were having problems.

Jon testified that one day Boland came into his office with a bag of garbage and said he found it in the dumpster next to Jon's office and asked him why he hadn't ripped it up. Then he threw the garbage on the office floor and walked out.

Jon said they had never been instructed to rip up garbage and furthermore, when he examined it more closely he saw that it wasn't even from his center, but had been imported from a different center.

Jon also testified that Jim Barry would come and sit in his office, which was about 12 by 15 feet, and "just sit in a chair and stare at me and watch me do my work. He wouldn't speak. He wouldn't ask any questions. He'd just sit there and stare at me for a half hour, 45 minutes, get up, walk out; maybe an hour later come back, just sit there and stare again. I had no idea—at that point I was very scared to even ask the man what he was doing there."

During this period, the couple said they had received a lot of crank calls at home, and Patti found notes in her car about her moral ethics. One of the male managers admitted to Jon that he had written some of them. In August, Jon said in his testimony, he was summoned to Jim Barry's office once more, and was told he was going to be transferred from Bound Brook to Parsippany, where he would be made manager of the Dover center. His supervisor also said that he would have liked to see Jon get a job with more responsibility, but again, because of his relationship with Patti, that was out of the question. Then Barry said, "You gave up your career for the love of a woman, and as long as you continue this relationship, you will never be considered for a promotion or more responsible position."

Jon Slohoda obediently reported to the new center. The offices were in the same district as the old office and Jon was given the "silent" treatment here, too. None of his fellow management people, he says, would speak to him. Did his fellow workers behave this way out of dumb obedience? Were they afraid of being fired? Or did it tap into the primitive pleasure people get from being able to vent their personal frustrations on a scapegoat?

Jon had been at the new center for two and a half months when he arrived at work one day in November 1981 and was accused of falsifying company records. UPS did fire Jon Slohoda. They said they fired him because he falsified company records. In the court and in statements to the press, UPS said he was fired only because he falsified records—a charge he denied.

Did someone falsify evidence? The time cards were exhibited in court and it was agreed by both sides that several of them had been altered. Who did it? It seems highly unlikely that such a successful manager for ten years, who had been number one in production ratings, and who was obviously in company disfavor, needed to botch up any records, or would take that chance when he was under constant scrutiny. No proof has been presented to implicate either side.

However, Division Manager Robert McGuire, in responding to questions, admitted that someone with Jon's experience would have to *want* to get caught and fired to make the alterations he was accused of making:

Q: Jon mentioned and you agreed . . . that it would be dumb to alter these reports as it was part of an experiment that everyone was watching and as there were double time records being kept . . . it would be easy to get caught. Is that correct?

A: That's correct.

Q: And at the time you stated that you thought he was trying to get caught and fired. Is that correct?

A: That's correct.

Q: Why did you think he was trying to get caught and fired?

A: Because of the obviousness of the corrections, the alterations.

And in a sworn affidavit, Daniel Delaney, who was center manager in Bernardsville, said that James Barry told him on several occasions, "We will get him sooner or later." At a conference in October 1981, Joseph Schneider, regional personnel director of UPS, told Delaney, according to his affidavit, that "they intended to get rid of Jon." When Jon was terminated, Barry said in front of Delaney and several other managers, according to the affidavit, "that UPS had to get rid of him, that the company could not tolerate relationships between employees such as occurred between Slohoda and Arnett."

Jon had been branded an adulterer, but he was discharged, UPS claimed, for something else. Had Jon not been technically married when he was making love to someone else, it would evidently have been accepted. As his lawyer, Nancy Erika Smith, later said, "What UPS is saying is that adultery is morally reprehensible but fornication is not."

While UPS denied that Jon's extramarital relationship had anything to do with their firing him, they counteracted Jon's suit initially in the 1983 motion for dismissal by arguing that even if that had been the reason for the discharge, they would have had the right to fire him at will, and that adulterers are not protected by the state law forbidding marital discrimination.

In referring to New Jersey's antidiscrimination statute, UPS's attorney, Marvin Frankel, sharply disagreed with Slohoda's contention and told the court, "It is absurd to believe that that statute was meant to protect anybody from being fired for adultery. When that statute was written or amended to include marital status in 1970, adultery was a crime in New Jersey and to say that the legislature meant to protect an adulterer because to discriminate against them was discriminating on the grounds of marital status is ludicrous." Slohoda's lawyer, Nancy Erika Smith, says the law was on the books but hadn't been enforced for years.

The case brought up a number of questions. Do nepotism rules cover people who are living together but unmarried or only married people? The Appeals Court noted that the New Jersey courts have not decided whether an antinepotism policy is applicable to an employee living with, but not married to, a co-employee. They also warned courts to be cautious about dismissing a case on a meager record "where the ruling sought . . . would have a broad social and legal effect." Can single people fornicate without reprisal while married people who are doing the same thing cannot because that is adultery, which some managers feel is wrong. And what, if anything, does company policy say about all this? Further, are personal moral judgments being mistaken by supervisors for corporate policy?

According to the UPS brief, they believe that "the rationale for prohibiting two spouses from working together supports . . . a policy of not allowing two unmarried employees who become engaged in a sexual, romantic or espoused relationship to remain in the company's employ."

This opens the question, it seems to me, of how such a company is going to safeguard itself in these situations. Will people report on their friends and colleagues? Will jealous co-workers who want to get rid of someone give management false statements about fictitious affairs? Will companies be forced to hire detectives to spy on their executives?

The UPS brief makes note of Slohoda's assertion that unmarried UPS employees have lived together without being dismissed and says, "Even if [Slohoda's] faulty factual premise is accepted, his proposed conclusion is without merit. Our society, rightly or wrongly, has distinguished steadily between fornication and adultery. Unless some law forbade this, UPS's management was privileged to do likewise. . . . It makes no difference that some might deem the asserted position of [UPS] outmoded or 'old-fashioned.' This is not a case to adjudicate sexual morals. It is a claim by [Slohoda] of a 'right' not to be fired for adultery. The case should end here because there is no such right."

Jon Slohoda and Patti Arnett were married in September 1983. After a six-month search, Jon finally found a new job, but it is not a comparable one. For a while Patti continued working at UPS, but Jon says they treated her terribly, transferring her often from day shift to night shift and from one location to another, while "giving her the cold shoulder." She finally decided to sue UPS for discrimination and harassment. The case was settled out of court and she has not yet found a new job.

I spoke with Nancy Erika Smith, Jon Slohoda's attorney, about the legal ramifications of the case. How far can an employer go in dictating the private love life of its employees? She pointed out that most states are "employment at will" states, which means employers can hire and fire whomever they want as long as they don't violate any law. Smith alleges UPS violated New Jersey's law which makes it illegal to make detrimental employment decisions on the basis of sex, race, age, marital status, handicap, religion, national origin, color, birth defects, or cellular traits. However, the marital clause is more unusual, and while states like New York and California have it, others may not.

UPS argued that firing someone because he was an adulterer did not violate the law against discrimination. In his January 1983 ruling Judge Rumana had agreed with them that the legislature did not mean to protect adulterers. But when Smith brought the case before the Appellate Division, its three-judge panel, in January 1984, found unanimously in favor of Slohoda and against UPS. In its judgment, firing someone for adultery could possibly constitute discrimination.

The court also questioned the kind of surveillance necessary to enforce a corporation's rules about employees' private lives. Was the state constitution's law on privacy violated? Under the New Jersey constitution, the right to privacy is guaranteed under the first article and is specifically stated. There is, by the way, no longer a law in New Jersey against adultery. It was repealed in 1978.

"I think UPS is trying to paint with a very broad brush to establish an incredibly far-reaching right to fire whomever they want," said Smith. "I think someone like Jon Slohoda, who they admit was a very good employee—his center was the best in the district, not one blemish on his record after ten years with the company—should not be able to be fired because they don't like what he does with his private life." She also finds the company pretty hypocritical. "Here is a corporation where Jon said he went out with the very people who fired him, and they would always make sexist comments about women in the bars and about Patti before they knew the two were living together." Suddenly, his interest in sex with just one woman was intolerable.

Commenting on the case, Smith questioned the corporation's judgment. "Jon Slohoda was an exemplary employee by their standards. He had moved up faster than anyone else in the North Jersey district. It's as though they had to root out certain people who didn't fit their moral standards. What kind of surveillance will be needed to enforce that rule? Will they follow people home?" she asked. "Are they going to make people sign statements about who they are and are not sleeping with? It raises a lot of very serious issues about people's private lives."

The case of Jon Slohoda is not a fluke. Smith says UPS employees in Illinois, California, and New York have also been fired for adultery. And when publicity on the case appeared in the news, she received calls from all over the country from discharged workers and lawyers who were involved with similar cases.

As in the example of Gina versus IBM, UPS made a great

mistake. In Gina's case, a tragedy occurred because of mismanagement due to lack of experience and bad judgment by several
individuals, rather than as a response to firm company policy. In
Jon's case, company policy evidently found his personal behavior
objectionable. In either instance, the cost to the company was the
loss of one of its first-rate managers, the expense of lawyers and
a trial, and a lot of bad publicity.

Those at the top who think they can control the moral, ethical,
sexual, and personal codes of the people who work for them are
being challenged. Employers are not our parents, our ministers,
or our judges. And they buy only a portion of our lives.

## NO LIVING TOGETHER—
## CASALETT *v.* FOOTE & DAVIES

Though Jon Slohoda and his wife separated, technically he was
married when he started living with his lover. People do that every
day. But UPS did not approve. Now, if neither of the two lovers
was married, could a corporation possibly object? If they did not
work for competing companies? If they worked in completely
separate departments? Indeed they could—and do.

In the process of doing research for this book, I spoke to a
woman named Elizabeth Casalett. She told me what I felt was
a rather hair-raising story about her employment at a printing
company called Foote & Davies, headquartered in Atlanta,
Georgia. At that time it was a subsidiary of J. P. Stevens, but it
has since become independent. Liz decided to sue her former
employer because she felt she was unjustly fired, and her lawyer
filed a complaint in the Superior Court of the State of California
in San Mateo County on October 17, 1983. But before the case
could be heard, Foote & Davies suggested an out-of-court settlement which Liz accepted. Part of the stipulation was that no one
involved with the case, including the lawyers for both sides, was
permitted to discuss it. This meant my detailed interview with Liz

had to be stricken from this book, since Liz could not sign a release.

However, from the two available sources, her legal complaint, which is in the public record, and a brief appearance on the November 1, 1984, segment of the TV program *20/20*, produced by ABC News, the bare bones of the story can be discerned. I leave the fleshing out to the imagination of the reader.

In April 1982, Elizabeth went to work for Foote & Davies in Brisbane, California. She was hired as their general accounting manager. The firm was to provide her with benefits and promotional opportunities "equal to or greater" than those offered by the company's competitors and "equal to or greater" than those offered the male employees, according to her contract. In addition, they were not to discriminate against her on the basis of her sex, pregnancy, or marital status, and not to fire her without good cause.

According to her complaint, she performed admirably and "rendered service to [Foote & Davies] far in excess of the level required." Elizabeth received a 40 percent raise in salary during her first year of employment as well as two performance reviews indicating her work was commendable.

A year later, in March 1983, Larry Rigby, the corporate controller, and Bert Steele, a cost accounting manager, discovered that Liz had met and presumably fallen in love with Tim Casalett, a manager in a different part of the company. Foote & Davies, according to Liz's complaint, had "conducted an investigation of [Liz] when she left her workplace and conducted surveillance of her private life." What this detective work uncovered was that Liz was receiving flowers in the office from Tim once a week and they were living together.

In order to find out who was sending flowers to their employee, they had asked the company janitor, who also happened to be the janitor of the flower shop, to do some snooping. Liz assumes that once they knew who was sending the flowers, they matched up telephone numbers and realized the two were sharing a house.

Tim told his *20/20* interviewer that he didn't want the company to know about their personal lives, and that they had gone out of their way to not tell anyone that they were dating or even going out with each other.

Nevertheless, when the investigation showed that Liz and Tim were having a romance, her boss threatened that she would be fired if she did not end the relationship.

Her complaint also charged that Foote & Davies prepared and disseminated reports about her private, off-the-job conduct, which was "of no legitimate concern to Foote & Davies," including information about her relationship with Tim, who was then her fiancé. At that point, Frank Kutcher, president of the company, who was in the Atlanta office, ordered her fired "for immoral behavior."

Steele began to tell a number of Liz's fellow employees that she was engaged in "immoral conduct," that she "slept around," and that she was not loyal to the company.

Someone apparently had second thoughts, because a month later, Bryant Whittaker, chief operating officer of the San Francisco office, met with Liz and Tim and apologized to them. He told them they were not immoral, that they would not be fired, that their jobs were secure as long as their work was satisfactory. He also told them he thought their job performance was more than satisfactory at that time.

The following month, on May 15, Liz and Tim were married. At the end of the month, Liz announced that she was pregnant and wanted a maternity leave of up to three months beginning the following October. She never had a chance to receive it, because she was fired on August 8, despite the fact that she had an outstanding record, was Foote & Davies's highest ranking woman executive, and was seven-and-a-half months pregnant. Her lawyer said this action violated her right to privacy guaranteed in the state constitution, her right to employment without discrimination (a violation of the California Government Code), her right to take a maternity leave (having been there for a year she was entitled to maternity benefits), and her freedom of association.

Liz asked Foote & Davies for a copy of the medical insurance policy which covered her during her employment and also the proper forms for converting her group employees' insurance to individual insurance. Although, as her complaint said, her supervisors knew she would incur substantial medical expenses because of her pregnancy, they did not send her copies of the insurance or conversion forms within the conversion deadline. She thus could not get insurance to cover her pregnancy-related expenses.

In addition, after firing her, her company did not give her the same severance benefits that male employees in similar positions received. The complaint charged Foote & Davies with "willful, wanton, malicious, and oppressive" behavior. In short, Liz's employer was accused of not acting in good faith, of slander, invasion of privacy, and harassment because she was cohabiting with a man to whom she was not married, and firing her to avoid having to pay benefits for the three-month duration of her pregnancy leave. Her supervisors also refused to allow Liz to review her entire personnel file, in violation of the Labor Code, and they removed her performance reviews from the file before finally letting her see it.

In their answer to the complaint, Foote & Davies and the defendants employed by that company denied "each and every allegation" made, said there were not enough facts to warrant a case, that they did act in good faith, and asked for the complaint to be dismissed. Now, had this case come to trial, all the details of the alleged discriminatory actions would have become publicly known. For some motive known only to them, Foote & Davies cut short the legal process by offering Liz the out-of-court settlement. This settlement offer could be an admission of guilt on the part of the company or it could mean only that they didn't want to bother spending the time and money and, although innocent, would rather pay off their former employee. Judging from the fact that Liz filed a charge of discrimination with the United States Equal Employment Opportunity Commission and the California Department of Fair Employment and Housing, which issued her a "right to sue" letter, there was enough evidence to be heard.

According to her complaint, Liz was obviously badly treated by everyone from her supervisors up to the president of the company, who felt they had the right to judge their employees' morals. Work performance, once again, had nothing to do with their punitive actions. The cost to this corporation was high. It lost an excellent worker, one who loved her job and the company itself and who wanted to stay. And the problem stems, once again, from the assumption of many companies that they can dictate how their employees should lead their private lives.

It might startle companies like these to know that two million *unmarried* men and women live together in the United States, according to a 1983 report from the Bureau of the Census—double what it was five years ago.

Now, although this figure represents only 4 percent of all U.S. couples, according to Dr. Charles F. Westoff, director of Princeton University's Office of Population Research, it seriously underestimates the number who have at one time or another lived this way. He estimates that the proportion of single men and women who have ever cohabited is more likely to be 25 percent of all couples.

Thus, for supervisors to try to impose a set of unrealistic rules on adult employees, men and women with superior education, background, and experience, many of whom do not yet wish to marry but who need completeness in their lives, or who need several years of normal dating and living together before marrying, is absurd. It will lead either to even more exacerbated disruption, or more frequent court cases. You cannot ask people to behave like celibate nuns and monks simply because they work for you.

## OTHER SEXUAL TALES

There are similar examples of Dark Ages morality everywhere in the country. Sometimes, as we have seen, the company can harass its employees, but other times it is simply a matter of requiring employees to follow a set of antiquated rules, written or unwritten, and expelling them if they don't.

Chicago lawyer Alan Mills told me about a client of his who was fired from a local underwriting company without being told why. Mills explained that in the two weeks prior to the firing, the man had begun sharing a house with a woman who also works for his company.

There appears to have been an unwritten policy against such things in this company, said Mills, of which this man was unaware. The woman who lived with him did not work for him but was in another department. He met her on one of his business trips, and she transferred to his company in Chicago, where she was fortunate enough to get a job. They didn't announce that they were living together, but her expense accounts and moving bills had his address on them.

He was not aware of any office disruption caused by their cohabiting. He had recently been promoted and had gotten a raise. The lovers lived together for two weeks before he was fired.

One day when he made his usual call to pick up messages, he was told that he was needed at the office right away. He came in and was told, "Get your stuff out by tonight." When he asked why, the reply was, "No comment." His friend still works for the company.

Illinois has a constitutional provision and a statute which prohibit discrimination based on marital status. Said Mills, "Nobody has denied our allegation that if these two people had married, he would not have been fired."

In El Toro, California, John Moultak, twenty-seven, a Marine Corps pilot and a legal officer with an unblemished eight-year record, fell in love with Lance Corporal Candy Clark, twenty-two. The couple planned to marry and had told their superiors months before, hoping she could get an early discharge. Instead of receiving a blessing, Moultak was court-martialed and given a dishonorable discharge for conduct unbecoming an officer. The couple bitterly remarked that an officer who had beaten and raped Clark the previous year had been honorably discharged with full benefits. Are love and marriage less honorable than assault and rape?

In another instance, when a phone-call tracking system at a New York financial services company showed a series of long-distance calls from an executive's extension to the home of another executive, it began a bit of corporate detective work into the private lives of those involved. The company discovered that the first executive was having an affair with the wife of the second, and he was immediately fired.

Another situation involved a woman who married her boss. They both worked for a 1,000-employee Fortune 500 subsidiary company. She guessed that about five people knew of their relationship. They decided to "go legit" and tell the company of their marriage. They were told it was fine. A few months passed and then, quite unexpectedly, she was fired. She said, "I lost the dream job of a lifetime when top management did a 180-degree turnabout on their original laissez-faire decision toward us as a married management team." In her letter to a woman's magazine, she wrote, "My husband still works for the company and has regained the personal and professional ground he lost. I was transferred and demoted over a trifling matter in which a subordinate lied. I found a better executive position within a week, but have still had some trouble readjusting. It has all been worth it, but we paid heavy penance for tawdry sins we did not commit—it reinforced my conviction that we weren't alone as victims of confused, frightened management."

Wharton's Professor Jerome Katz tells of another case in which he acted as a consultant. His client was a woman executive in a multinational corporation. She fell in love with her opposite number overseas. Somehow, they were discovered. It was a traditional corporation, so "when the boom came down, it came down on her," said Katz.

Her boss called her in and said, "We hear you are involved with a man in the company overseas, and we think you should resign." The couple had not made any efforts to hide their relationship.

The woman did not fight back. After a lot of soul-searching, she found a much better job in Europe close to her lover. She probably had a court case, said Katz, though the company did have an orally stated policy about discouraging relationships at work. Professor Katz thought she got a "dirty deal."

The ironic thing was that the two lovers did not see each other more often than perhaps twice a year in the course of business. They weren't dependent on each other's work, and they didn't influence each other's jobs. They were at the same level but in different structures. Once more, it was, as Katz says, "tradition in society and in the company, as well as the norms of the top management group and the industry," that was being enforced.

In our Constitution a strict rule insists on the separation of church and state. One does not dictate to the other. The separation of powers extends to the Supreme Court, Congress, and the president. They all have their independent functions. This separation of the forces of influence which govern our country and make policy is necessary to prevent any one faction gaining unfair advantage over the others, thus destroying any hope of honest decision making. In other words, it guarantees democracy. And the same logic should apply to business.

As New York's mayor Ed Koch remarked recently after appointing a homosexual judge despite objections, "The government does not belong in the bedrooms of the nation." One might add, with equal conviction, nor do corporations belong in the bedrooms of their employees. That proscription includes the current corporate penchant for dictating codes of conduct, morals, and lifestyles. Corporations that base their hiring and firing on their top executives' own moral standards are out-of-bounds. In most cases such practices are probably illegal, discriminatory, and harassing. And more and more often they will be taken to the courts until, one hopes, they will disappear.

# Chapter 4

# THE NEW CORPORATE PRESSURES

*W*hether one is working for an enlightened corporation or an unenlightened one, there are some new, universal pressures which are being brought to bear upon employees in the now coeducational workplace. People are groping for a way to blend their personal business with the business of the corporation. Forced into a state of involuntary schizophrenia by the attitudes of companies that are unprepared for this new development, most executives respond to the new pressures with fear and confusion.

When confronted with so human a problem as emotion, executives are not sure what to do and no one can tell them, since their superiors are usually suffering from the same discomfort as they themselves are. They need to know how to deal with romance when it exists in the executive office, and later, how to manage it if it breaks up. They sense the problem of favoritism that could result from affection. And they are aware of the notion that women rushing up the success ladder are often suspected of slipping between the bedsheets to get there. They are made uncomfortable by the many awkward moments when traveling with members of the other sex, or going to conventions with them. And they realize the terrible hurt that follows a company decision to play chaperone and break up a romance. They wonder whether to try to avoid such pain by keeping their love a secret, or whether such a thing is even possible to do. They are aware of the instant perceptions that come to mind the minute a man and woman are seen together, even if they are doing something as sexless as reading an annual report. And they are trying to figure out how to cope with the new questions of loyalty when men and women are married to each other as well as to their corporation.

The intensity of pressure will vary from one corporation to another, but even in the more liberal companies, many people feel the need to play some form of anxiety-producing hide-and-seek. For example, take the following two stories.

Sally, a young, single, attractive woman who was an officer in a large, world-renowned financial services company, became friendly with Tom, a young, single, attractive man who was also an officer. When the project they had worked on together was finished, they and another man decided to go out for a celebratory bash. At the last minute, the other man canceled, and the two went out alone. Their relationship began.

"Before, both of us had a really strong code of never getting involved with anyone at work. It was just too complicated. But we had a very good, close friendship," Sally explained. "Nevertheless, I felt the pressure of trying to maintain my own professional credentials and stature, and the limitations that being an officer's girl friend might impose." However, they did not normally work in the same building or the same division, which made things easier.

They tried to keep their relationship a complete secret and were remarkably successful. A year later, when they married, no one knew. "We were very, very cautious," Sally explained. "If we met after work, we'd meet on the third subway car of the train." Their circumspection was at times distracting, tension producing, and upsetting. At other moments the charade became almost comical.

One day just before their marriage, they were shopping in a department store for furniture. "We were talking, and I thought he was standing next to me when I got on the elevator to go to the third floor. I was still talking to him as I got on. When I got out he wasn't there. I presumed he must have gotten shoved by the crowd and was coming up in the next elevator. Ten minutes later I was still alone in the bed section wondering what had happened. Could I have made a mistake? Is everything off? This is bizarre. Maybe he's changed his mind." Finally, distraught, she went downstairs, but Tom wasn't on the main floor either. At least twenty minutes had elapsed. She frantically went outside, and there he was, nervously standing in front of the store, waiting for her.

Tom explained that as he was getting into the elevator he spotted someone from their Personnel Department who was known as the company gossip. Despite the fact that the company had dropped its rule which said that if two employees married, one would have to resign, he still felt so sensitive about the issue that he had dashed out of the store to avoid a confrontation. There was a very strong grapevine in their organization, and neither of them wanted gossip.

"I wasn't sure it would have hurt my career, had they known," Sally said, "but I had worked so hard to establish independent credentials and respect that I didn't want to take any chances, so I understood why he had disappeared. Both of us had too much pride in our work to want to be gossiped about."

She explained that had they been closer in terms of spheres of influence, they might have been afraid of being fired, but they weren't, so it was merely a case of not having anyone think of them in any way other than as serious professionals. And they didn't want people intruding on their private lives.

They had gone to such pains to conceal their relationship that not even her secretary had guessed. Her fiancé called her every day, but even these communications were kept undercover. With the kind of advance planning worthy of two master spies, they had arranged that if she didn't answer the phone, he would hang up the moment someone else did, since her calls would automatically jump to a phone in the next office. "Every once in a while I'd hear the phone slammed down because the fellow in the next office got tired of picking up the line and having the person on the other end hang up. One day he said, 'I've really had it with that phone. Every time I answer, someone hangs up.' And I'd say, 'Oh, you're kidding. I wonder why.' " People finally learned they were married when it was announced in the newspaper.

Even afterwards, they established a strong code by which they kept very separate business lives. If someone said anything to him that might have influenced her, for example, he would go out of his way not to tell her about it.

These two executives fell in love while working together and lived with the stresses and anxieties of a relationship they felt they had to keep invisible. Although there was no stated company policy that would have threatened them, they sensed judgmental pressures strongly enough to go to all sorts of trouble to ensure that their relationship remain undiscovered, at times hiding from company colleagues as though they were doing something shameful and illegal. Preserving their professional integrity while fulfilling personal desires was no easy balancing act.

An even more difficult situation existed for another couple, two professionals whose employment by a major Fortune 500 company had overtones more tragic than comic. Sue and Jim were employees of one of the country's largest and most prestigious corporations. Sue still works there. Jim, who is much older, had worked for the corporation for many years before Sue was hired to work in Jim's group.

They had met before at professional meetings, and she knew him by reputation. They worked together for about a year before they started to see each other socially. Before long, they had fallen in love.

"I don't think there was any written rule," Jim said, "but we knew there was an unwritten rule that people who were engaged or married would not be allowed to work together. We did not expect the corporation to discharge anybody, but we were sure one of us would have to move if they found out about our relationship." Jim remembered how happy they were and how much their work improved after they began seeing each other. "I think the company got a tremendous increase in work out of us, because we were both very interested in what we were doing, and very interested in each other."

"So we deferred our marriage," Sue explained," and made sure our relationship was carried on in the most discreet way possible. We never showed affection at the office, and we never referred to things we did together away from work." They traveled to the same places fairly often as part of their job, and although they would have dinner together, they never shared a room.

"I'm quite sure people suspected that it was more than just a business relationship," Jim admitted, "but since we shared a project, it was natural to see us together all the time. I think the central issue is that we never talked about it."

Occasionally someone would ask Sue, "What about your relationship with Jim?" and she'd insist, "I don't really have anything to say about that. We work together." She'd never get into a discussion. "I think the people who were concerned that something was going on were higher-level people," Sue recalled, "and if we had forced them to consult us by talking about it, that would have been our undoing. They would have separated us. But because we hid it completely and were so discreet, they didn't have to confront it, and so they could accept it, even if they knew."

"One supervisor did speak to me," Jim said. "He warned, 'You realize, of course, that if there is anything happening, if you live with this woman or marry her, she will not be able to work for you.' He did not force me to say whether we were involved or not. One thing that made the situation acceptable, even to those who were suspicious," Jim said, "was that Sue is a truly outstanding performer, and was viewed that way by many people including my boss and many others in high places."

Although Jim was the one who did her performance appraisals and recommendations for salary increases, no one person in that organization made the entire decision. Jim had to meet with the other supervisors and they would have to agree that she deserved such things as a merit raise. Furthermore, he never demanded anything outrageous for her, despite the fact that he loved her. He requested increases for her equal to those the others got.

Year after year, Jim and Sue continued to work together and to take carefully calculated steps to maintain their secret double life. They muddled on in a limbo of sustained frustration because they could not marry, they were under an endless strain trying to be sure they didn't say anything that would give them away, and Sue could never confide in her office friends about her romance, as people normally do. They had to maintain an unnatural silence about this exciting part of their lives. They did not even allow themselves the luxury of leaving the office together.

They did not dare live together. They rented separate houses three miles apart and every night, in steamy summer weather or frigid snowdrifts, Jim would drive the three miles over to Sue's house, have dinner with her, and drive the three miles back home at the end of the evening, month after month, year after year, for six years.

Another price they paid was a social one. Neither one of them had much of a life except with each other. Because they didn't want to date other people, and their friends tended to be those they worked with or professional associates, had they gone out together in public, word of it would have gotten right back to the company. So they had no sense of a normal existence. They lived in cloistered solitude, dutifully obeying the corporate rules.

But there was another sad result of the choice they made. Sue had wanted to have children and felt that she had to be married to have them. Because they postponed their marriage, she put herself beyond the childbearing years.

Finally, Jim reached retirement age. The two became publicly engaged and announced their wedding plans. Why did these two executives live lives of excessive secrecy and deception? Says Sue, "Our jobs were such a big part of our lives, it would have been a horrible conflict to have to choose between giving up the work we loved and giving up the person we loved. Our way of solving it was to go underground, and to continue our personal relationship without the sanction of marriage."

But her lover's retirement was in sight. "If we had had to wait sixteen years instead of six," said Jim, "it might have put this thing in a different light. I don't know what we would have done then."

As the ratio of men to women in corporations changes, the charged atmosphere which surrounds corporate romance may change too, and the Sues and Jims of the future may not have to suffer. But some of the problems will remain because people will always be entertained by scandal and gossip.

Besides the emotional minefields, demographic constraints produce a fertile ground for trouble. In addition to the inequities of executive numbers—many men and few women—one should consider such things as age, at which levels there are similar numbers, and the marital and career status of those at various junctures of the company hierarchy. Korn/Ferry International, an executive search firm, and the UCLA Graduate School of Management completed a study in 1982 of 300 senior-level women executives from the largest U.S. companies and came up with some statistics which, when compared with results from their 1979 study of male executives, show, I think, that the middle-aged man is quite vulnerable to a potential office romance.

According to Korn/Ferry, only 48 percent of the women executives were married (others were divorced, separated, or single) whereas almost all, or 95 percent, of the male executives had wives. And whereas among these married female executives, most (82 percent) of their husbands work, among married male executives the majority (86 percent) have wives who do not work. This leaves a lot of women at home involved in a domestic life that does not interest their husbands, and they know little about their husband's work or concerns. And it leaves a lot of unmarried female executives who do know what's going on and who speak the same language as these men. The contrast between the older, more powerful men with their unexciting marriages and the attractive, bright, single women co-workers who are savvy and willing is likely to awaken the innate romantic interests of the older corporate population. These older men have also probably gone as far as their careers will take them and are prime candidates to become mentors to their young, ambitious colleagues.

## WHAT TYPE OF PERSON ARE YOU?

Many men and women would become interested in sexual liaisons in the office, some would actively seek it, others would go out of their way to avoid it. Categorizing people is always risky. But by analyzing behavior in this way, we can better understand the cast of characters who cause many of the sexual pressures we see in offices.

From studies conducted by Yale sociology professor Rosabeth Moss Kanter in 1977 of groups where females were the minority among males, as they often are in business settings, and from her own work, Dr. Shelley E. Taylor, professor of psychology at the University of California, Los Angeles, devised the following categories of women according to how they behaved and how they were perceived by the men. Below is a list of how these categories might appear in an office.

MOTHER: This woman is a consoler of men, who seek her out to share confidences and get help and advice in solving their personal problems. They never think of her in any sexual way.
PRINCESS: She is special, sensitive, and easily hurt, and one man will join with her to protect her from other men.
SEDUCTRESS: A familiar type, she is overtly sexual and enjoys flirting to gain attention and power.

**IRON MAIDEN:** A cold, aloof, possibly dangerous woman. She probably would kill her own mother, or you, to get ahead.
**PET:** A group mascot who applauds male achievement and gains acceptance by being cute. She is smart, but tries not to show it so that men will like her.
**MS. EFFICIENCY:** Superorganizer, she may make men feel inadequate and uncomfortable, and rather than being attractive to them, she may well frighten them away.

To these groups, I would add four of my own, which can be male or female, although most of the first types are women.

**POWER SEEKERS:** These people respond to others with power to such an extent that they are apt to fall in love with the power per se rather than the person, and will confuse the two.
**ROMANTIC FOOLS:** These are men and women who care about their careers but refuse to put work ahead of romance, feeling they've got to grab love where they can find it. They expect others to understand, but in the current climate, they may hurt their careers.
**BUSINESSLIKE LOVERS:** Men and women who fall in love, usually keep it secret, manage it well so there are no disruptive waves even if others are suspicious, and are so businesslike in their demeanor that they are able to keep their work their primary concern when they are in the office.
**NEVER-MIXERS:** Those who never mix business and pleasure. They won't allow themselves to have a relationship because they are afraid of hurting their careers.

Dr. Terence McGuire, a psychiatrist and consultant to NASA's space program, has also identified the varied cast of characters in offices today and labeled those who are at greater risk than others of having an affair. From his psychiatrist's viewpoint, he describes them as follows:

**PROMOTERS:** those charming, adaptable, resourceful people who excel at talking others into things, selling ideas, products, or themselves. For them the excitement of the affair is the turn-on.

**REBELS:** the spontaneous, playful, creative people who don't like the autocratic or authoritarian approach to things. These people are turned on by the physical fun or play and the physical contact.

**REACTORS:** the "feeling" type, who are warm, compassionate, and sensitive. These people are turned on by the shared emotional investment, and a greater need for sensuous input such as hugs, touches, or tenderness.

Those who are at much less risk of a corporate romance, according to this psychiatrist, are the workaholics, the "persisters" with their dedicated, conscientious approach, who can sometimes be opinionated and righteous, and the "dreamers," who are reflective, imaginative, but rather passive.

Now obviously some of these categories overlap. Dr. Taylor's Seductress probably would appear at first to be one of Dr. McGuire's Rebels. But here we can do some fine tuning. This Seductress might conceivably be a Promoter or a Reactor, depending on why she is being so sexual. And she might also fit into my group and be a Power-seeker. It all depends on her motivation, her style, and what she is looking for. After all, a Seductress who is a Rebel as well as a Power-seeker might, once having landed her man, switch over and protect herself by agreeing to become a Businesslike lover.

The fact that employees come in a variety of mental and emotional mixes creates the complicated office populations we hear more and more about. It is why men and women can be creative when working together, but it is also why when you add women to men in corporate offices the pressures increase exponentially, causing a surprising array of policy problems. Fear of scandal and demographic and personality pressures are but a few of the many dilemmas that affect any pair of executives who decide to have a relationship.

## CAN YOU KEEP IT SECRET?

One of the major pressures executives face when they undertake an office romance is to make the decision whether or not to keep it a secret. After that, they must live with the tensions they inherit when they make one choice or the other. There is also the very practical question of whether or not it is psychologically possible to keep love a secret.

Professor John Gabarro of Harvard's Graduate School of Business Administration said, "I suspect there are a lot of people who do fall in love with each other, understand the immediate negative consequences of their colleagues' knowing it, are extraordinarily discreet, and are not discovered."

A publishing executive said she thought it was possible to keep an affair a secret. "I was in a company once," she said, "and after I left I found out that the marketing director had slept with three different women, and I'd never guessed. He was a friend of mine. I hadn't noticed anything."

A marketing director remembered, "I called someone at a subsidiary of ours and I mentioned that I was living with a friend, and this person said, 'Gee, are you so open about it?' He explained to me that he'd been living with someone who worked for our corporation in Canada, and then married her. But they'd kept it top secret. They would come and leave in separate cars. I thought that it could be like the old story of the sociological study in the small Southern town where everybody said it's wrong to drink, and it turned out that when somebody went around to check, practically everybody had beer in their refrigerator. But nobody wanted to let anybody know because they thought everybody would disapprove."

## THE NEW CORPORATE PRESSURES

This is probably also true of office romance. Afraid of stunting their careers or being gossiped about, many people are probably successfully hiding affairs from others who also may be romantically involved. Leading this kind of deceptive life, in addition to the stress of normal work, must create an unbearable extra tension that is unfortunate, and should not be necessary if people are doing their jobs. If the "beer in the refrigerator" syndrome is operative here, too, it would be more than unfortunate. It would be downright farcical.

Many would say such efforts at camouflaging one's real activities are a waste of time. They say you cannot hide such a strong emotion as love, and even if you think you are successfully concealing it, you are deluding yourself, fooled by the fact that your colleagues reward your discretion by saying nothing. An advertising executive said he had seen many affairs in his agency. "If you work with anybody for any length of time, he or she will have very basic work patterns. As soon as someone deviates from that, it doesn't take a lot of brains to figure out what's going on. When you see *two* people deviating and they happen to be crossing paths a lot, you know."

A similar viewpoint was expressed by another executive, "I don't think people can keep an affair secret. Living in a corporation, you spend forty to fifty hours a week with these people. There isn't much you don't know about them. You may be able to closet away an alcoholic spouse, but usually they find out. They find out that your kid is having problems in school, or had an accident. It's like living in the same house. People find out."

Another person told of a woman in his office who was having an affair, but was married. Her friend was with the company in another part of the country, and she had him send his letters to the office. One day her secretary was out and she had a temporary. This woman opened a personal letter, not realizing she shouldn't have.

"They'd have to be awfully good actors to hide an affair," said a pharmaceutical company director.

I asked Dr. Ellen Berscheid, professor of psychology at the University of Minnesota, what she thought: can you keep love a secret? "No, I don't think so," she said. "It's a hard secret to keep, because one's manner toward the other person changes; the non-verbals change." For example, she said those in love are constantly aware of the other's presence and one will change posture when the other comes into the room. In some cases those in love change their manner, not necessarily toward the other person, but in general.

Management consultant Rick Driscoll, of the Driscoll Consulting Group in Massachusetts, believes people should be discreet but it would be "the height of naiveté to expect for a minute that people don't know about it." Fellow consultant Jeanne Bosson Driscoll said, "Even if it's a one-sided relationship, people see it: 'Oh, I noticed you raised your left eyebrow when so-and-so walked into the room.'"

Karen Brethower, a consultant and former vice president and director of manpower development at Chase Manhattan Bank, said she has seen more than one instance where a woman has become involved with a married man and thinks that it's invisible, whereas in fact it's very, very visible and her career suffers as a result. Both people's judgment is seen to be questioned, or they are not given sensitive assignments, even within the same job.

She points out that it can be bad for one's career in the sense that "people can't say, 'I know you are having an affair with someone but you haven't made it public, but would you consider moving to Seattle?' So what happens is the person doesn't even get asked."

Cincinnati management consultant Nancy Brown says, "I think if two people have any kind of consistent relationship, others will pick up the vibes. I remember being in a meeting when I was working for a corporation," she said, "and there was a fairly high-level manager in the room plus a number of others and a woman colleague of mine.

"We walked out of that meeting, and she and I were driving back to another office and I said to her, 'Are you involved with him?' And she was flabbergasted. She said, 'How did you guess?' And I said, 'Here are the signals I saw: the way you looked at each other, the tone of voice when you spoke, the body language.' People pick up on the attraction."

She also commented that keeping a romance secret until one is sure may put a funny kind of torque on the relationship itself. "I'm not sure how healthy it is to try to grow an intimate friendship in secret, because most of them, certainly serious ones, exist in a social context. The minute you go public it sheds a different kind of light and heat on the relationship that could destroy it."

Despite the fact that most people seem to feel secrecy is a hard state in which to be convincing, most of those who get involved try to stay undercover. In Professor Quinn's study, described earlier, two thirds of the couples first attempted to keep their alliance hidden because of fear of breaking company rules and being punished, fear of gossip and general disapproval, or, if married, fear that the wife or husband would find out.

He too found that despite such efforts at discretion, the lovers often failed. The most common tip-offs, according to his study, were being seen together away from work, spending an unusual amount of work time chatting, taking long lunches, having long discussions behind closed doors, and taking joint business trips. Less subtle but surprisingly common signs, says Professor Quinn, involve the physical expression of affection. In about one third of his cases the couple was seen embracing in closets, kissing in supply rooms, or fondling in the parking lot.

Even after the couple is found out, in half the cases, according to the study, although everyone knows, and everyone knows that everyone knows, the couple will continue to act as if the relationship didn't exist, and their colleagues will continue to pretend that they don't know. He said some relationships have a legitimizing effect and give others the courage to try the same thing. In

22 percent of the cases, when found out, a romance inspired others to try liaisons of their own.

The tendency to try to keep romance concealed is understandable, and there seems to be a universal feeling among those involved that they can manage it. If they stick their heads in the sand, no one will see them. Like those in certain industries such as banking, advertising, and law, who seem inclined to take cover under an umbrella of secrecy until they at least know they are serious, others in different industries have also felt it even more crucial to their careers to hide their affections. Management consultant Kaleel Jamison says, however, that even though people who are romantically involved often have the fantasy that nobody knows, as Professor Quinn discovered, it is wishful thinking because people usually know a lot.

She spots the clues easily while consulting inside corporations, clues that shine out like traffic lights. For instance, lovers often talk very quietly on the phone with their backs turned to the door. They might avoid walking down a hallway with someone they might normally be very friendly with. Or she might spot them being inarticulate around each other. "Now, granted this is my work," she acknowledged, "but if I see it going on when I'm there only once a month, then others in the organization who observe each other closely every day must be picking it up. I've always been aware," she continued, "that the vibrations from sexual energy are very apparent. There is so much going on in organizations at all levels that people become very sharp and astute at paying attention to the subtleties."

She gave me an example of a case in which the secret was out and the couple thought they were still operating undercover. Roger was an executive in marketing and sales for a manufacturing company. His office had a glass window that faced the main office, where a group of sales representatives sat in a room like a bullpen. One day Roger was talking to one of the men who reported to him and he said, "Mary and I are getting married next month."

And the fellow said, "Yeah, we all knew it was coming sooner or later."

Roger said, "You couldn't have known! We've been incredibly discreet. We have not been seen in public. There is no way you could have known."

The fellow said, "We did know. We've known since the first week you started dating her."

Roger said, "That's impossible."

His subordinate explained. "The way we knew is that one Monday you came into the office, and your usual pattern was to stop and look at the sales board before you went into your office, but you didn't do that. You went directly into your office and made a phone call, while turning your back to us. We all commented on it. The next day you came in and did the same thing, turned your back and made a phone call. And we noticed that you punched out four numbers on your phone, so we knew it was an inside call.

"On Wednesday you came in and did the same thing. But by Wednesday we had divided up the phone book into sections, so that when you started your call, we went into action, and we called all the numbers in the phone book. We narrowed it down to three numbers, because those were the only ones that were busy. On Thursday you did it again, and we checked it out and had the person identified. So by Friday we were sure that's what was happening."

Obviously this kind of detective work would be possible only in a small company, and this one had very clever people who, says Jamison, "discovered very creative ways of finding out what people are doing."

Assuming some people can be successfully secretive for a while, how does that kind of covert living affect them? According to San Francisco psychiatrist Dr. Brian Gould, "On one hand it is stressful; on the other it is delicious. It's fun at first; then after a while the effort gets wearing, and people are likely to give up and come out in the open."

He says one of the critical variables in how it affects the individual is what the job means to that person. "How much is this a part of their identity, versus how much is it seen by them as something they do for money?" The more they professionally identify with the job, he points out, the more stress they would be under to prevent any problem that would jeopardize their standing. And the higher you go on the corporate ladder, the more the job becomes your identity. It determines where you live, how you live, the amount of money you have, and how much prestige and esteem you enjoy.

"If I behave in a way that would make me lose my standing as a professional or a physician," he explains, "I lose more than just a job. I lose my identity. When you look at what happens to physicians who lose their licenses, you find very high suicide rates, alcoholism, divorce, and other personal catastrophes."

He believes that the stress of a clandestine affair "can be very guilt-provoking and destructive to some individuals, but we also have to make mention of the fact that a few are invigorated by it. Some like the stress of secret meetings, glances during conferences, the possibility of having a hidden advantage, knowing others don't yet know but might find out. For that kind of person, the arousal of the affair itself may more important than the particular woman." One hastens to add: "or man."

## IS LOVE BLIND?

In March 1984, a story appeared in the news about a twenty-seven-year-old Tennessee lawyer named Mary Evans who fell so deeply in love with her thirty-seven-year-old client, a convicted murderer, that she helped him escape and fled with him. Four months later they were caught in Daytona Beach, Florida. She pleaded guilty and received a suspended sentence under an agreement whereby she would enter a mental hospital. One could certainly assume that the passions of love had indeed blinded lawyer Evans.

According to Dr. Gould, people do go crazy with love at the beginning. "Yes, love is not only blind," he says, "it makes you temporarily unfit for anything else—if you are talking about romantic, passionate love. But thankfully that stage usually doesn't last very long."

At the start of an affair, "one is going to be on the phone to one's 'honey' too often, and there's no getting around that. Spring fever is a very real phenomenon. But we all live with that," he said. "No business operates at one hundred percent efficiency, and never will." The corporation, it would seem, simply has to live with the consequences of love among its employees from time to time.

However, most of the executives I spoke with felt that people can fall in love decorously and professionally. One could be irrational for a brief period of time. The "blind" stage lasts for perhaps six months, according to Dr. Berscheid; an intense emotion is felt uniquely toward that one other person and can cloud decisions. But it is not always this way.

Dr. Meredith Titus, a psychologist with the Menninger Foundation, thinks it is possible to be in love and make sensible decisions. "What happens more often than not is that the couple will go overboard to avoid making it look like one is doing something special for the other." This can also affect the corporation adversely, she says, because someone who is really good might take a back seat so as not to appear to be favored, and the company could lose out.

Karen Brethower says she believes people can learn to handle their infatuations and love. "I think that's what you are going to find, as more and more men and women do share their future and their goals around business. It's a richer, deeper, and more intense relationship than many husbands and wives have because of the synergy that's there."

She says love does not necessarily have to make people irrational. Either they learn to incorporate this wonderful thing into their lives, or they are so immature that they can't handle it. "In that case," she says, "they are unsuited both for being in love and for being in business.

"I would say," she continued, "if people are in a loving relationship they are far more likely to be useful than cause trouble, because their life is working for them, and they can fully give themselves to their jobs."

Dr. Jennifer Macleod, who is a social psychologist and consultant, thinks that the mentally unbalanced, neurotic love from which people go crazy and think the love object is absolutely faultless happens in the first love of early youth, but it doesn't happen that often among mature adults. She said you might find it in those who are looking for a partner to complete themselves, people who cannot function independently, who need someone to fill the gaps in their lives. "That is a very immature attitude," she emphasized.

Though there are notable exceptions, it seems likely that the irrational love the sonnets idealized may have been more common in times when women were little more than sexual objects, and were expected to faint at the slightest rush of emotion or write passionate notes to their forbidden suitors. But love among intelligent, serious, career-minded men and women is less likely to be an affair of uncontrollable passion. Organizational men and women care too much about their careers to let that happen. The notion of blind love may be one of those ideas that is falling more and more into the realm of sexual mythology.

## CAN YOU TURN LOVE OFF?

If it is clear that a relationship might cause problems, yet the attraction lingers, is it possible to turn it off? And should one even try?

When I asked a publishing executive whether she thought it was better to go ahead and follow your heart, or refuse to allow yourself to have an affair if complications loom like iron-gray storm clouds, she said she didn't know. "I have such mixed feelings about this. I am a person who believes in following the heart. Love doesn't come along that often, and if you are in love with someone, I think you should go for it," she said. "Yet *job* is important, too. But all things considered, I think *heart* is more important than *job,* assuming you have a place to live and can pay the rent."

A director of human resources fell in love but did not have an affair, "because tapes in my head said, 'Unh-unh, don't fool around at work.' " The general counsel with whom she was traveling back and forth to Houston made advances, and she always used a sense of humor, or else hit it straight on. "I was scared to death because we were both married, and I tend to commit myself too easily. There really was a caring and there still is today. He is still married and I'm divorced, but we have a very special relationship because we share similar dreams of wanting to build the same kind of business. But it's scary," she admitted. "I think if he were under different pressures, we'd have a love affair."

She finally stopped his advances by saying, "Look, I can't handle this." They had a very direct conversation about it. Was she successful in turning her attraction off? Yes and no. They didn't have the affair, but the feelings remain. It is perfectly possible to be rational about it and say it doesn't make sense for this or that reason. She firmly believes that "we probably give in to attractions way too easily."

Many people think that if they have strong feelings of attraction for someone, they have to rush into an intimate relationship. Says management consultant Janice Eddy, "We should get to the point where we can acknowledge the attraction and then not go any further. Americans think if they feel something about someone, they've got to go all the way, that there must be some action."

That is an important point to keep in mind, in the opinion of many consultants. As Arleen LaBella puts it, "Our feelings and

our actions can be very different. It is reasonable to think there
will be attractions, and it is equally reasonable to think that we
never have to take any action on those feelings whatsoever. We
don't have to express them. We don't have to move any closer
toward that person in any way." She points out that if you are in
control, those feelings of attraction don't need to be a threat to
you. You can look at someone and say, "My, that's a terrific-
looking man," or, "That's a beautiful woman," and know that you
can handle it.

Janice Eddy tells of a woman in a large corporation who walked
into a manager's office to talk to him about a project they were
going to work on. They had seen each other at meetings and knew
one another casually. She sat down and he looked at her. The he
said, "Joanne, I can't carry on this meeting. I am so attracted to
you that I have to deal with myself about it. We'll reschedule the
meeting. I find it too difficult right now." He put the problem on
himself instead of her. He didn't try to talk it through with her.
She left his office realizing that she was both shocked and flat-
tered.

In a week or so the meeting was rescheduled and he was
friendly, pleasant, and professional. He never brought up the
subject again. He realized he had a choice and decided which way
he wanted to go. He found her attractive, but was grown-up
enough to turn his attraction off.

"Men have told me," says Eddy, "that when they meet a
woman they are drawn to, they fantasize even more than
women do, or at least it seems to bother them more, and they
have trouble having such fantasies without acting on them. It
becomes so real. Since men are used to taking action, the possibility that they can just enjoy what is in their minds without
doing anything about it, or without confusing it with reality, is
news to a lot of them."

She finds that men who handle the situation effectively are
those who talk with each other about it, and she thinks that is

critical. "Men don't have to feel guilty about their fantasies," she says. "It's perfectly normal to have them, and it's not being sexist. Some men are confused about that."

Psychiatrist Terence McGuire also says we do have choices. "A married person attracted to someone else might indeed shut off because of moral or ethical feelings about it. A lot of people make a straightforward decision, realizing, 'It's not good for me, and maybe not good for the other person.' That doesn't mean it's easy. They may go through a period of depression."

The director of the human sexuality program at the University of California in San Francisco, Dr. Evalyn S. Gendel, agrees that a woman or a man makes a conscious choice whether or not to become involved with someone with whom they work, especially the person determined to go up the corporate ladder. She says she sees fifteen to twenty women in prestigious jobs every month who would like to get to know the men they work with, but believe from the outset that they need to be pretty single-minded in their careers. These women choose to ignore such attractions, though it may be difficult.

She says people sometimes become angry or resentful about their situations, because at their particular point in life, their careers must have first priority.

Though one can turn love off, or at least prevent oneself from acting on loving feelings, there is another group, the risk-takers, who decide not to nip their affection in the bud. Says Dr. Gendel, "These people assume that if you feel attracted and the other person does too, you should pursue it in an open way." In either case, until a decision is made, "there can be real tension and psychological conflict between the career and the risk of becoming involved with someone at work. Some women who opt for love sometimes are badly burned because they allowed themselves to form trusting relationships only to find that the other person wanted a promotion or a transfer, that fact came first, and they were rejected."

"We still believe that sexual attraction is overwhelming. But sex doesn't take people over," says Dr. Gendel. "We do have control over it." Some people are very goal oriented. If they think a relationship is going to detract from work, they stay away. "There are some very determined people out there, both men and women."

## CAN YOU SURVIVE A BREAKUP?

A relationship rarely breaks up without someone getting hurt. The pressure of having to work with a former lover toward whom you may be bitter is often intense, and the emotions surrounding a failed romance can often be as disrupting as the romance itself. A junior partner in a very large law firm told the colleague he became engaged to, and then broke up with, that he would do everything in his power to get her fired because he could not stand the tension of working in the same place she did.

- A male executive worried, "If you were married, the woman could blackmail you after the affair was over."
- One woman said, "He might cut me off from information that I need to do my job properly."
- A lawyer thought it would be better to transfer. "It would be a lot easier if you weren't working together. It's painful to see the person. It can drive you crazy."
- A manager worried about getting so close during a relationship that you exchange a great deal of information. "If you break up, the other person could do a lot of damage to you."

I asked Dr. Macleod how people can manage their hurt and bitterness after a breakup and still do the job. "A lot of people work with others they despise and work effectively with them. So if you are a professional or a managerial person," she says, "that's one of the things you have to do. And if you can't, then you have a performance problem."

Such problems exist. One executive told about a top man in his office who had a blatant affair with the woman who ran the computer center. When the affair broke up, he was very nasty to her in public. They worked together and had to see each other. The atmosphere in the office became extremely strained.

In another case, when they found out about a couple's affair, the staff didn't say a word. It didn't bother anyone. If anything, they were all amused. But when the romance blew apart, it affected everyone. People avoided speaking to the couple or bringing the two people together, even if they needed to confer or resolve something.

This office gave a lot of presentations to clients, and when the man who gave the presentations and the woman who worked on all the graphics didn't cooperate, it was impossible to conduct business. He behaved so badly that he finally ended up transferring to another state.

For corporations, one of the more threatening aspects of the breakup of an affair is that the incident can degenerate into charges of sexual harassment, about which there are strict laws and penalties. In one example, a woman supervisor and a male subordinate in a state agency in the Midwest were having an affair. The affair fell apart, and the woman denied the man a promotion she had told him he would get. He then filed a suit for sexual harassment.

Take another case. A senior VP of a very large corporation, who was married with a family, had an affair with one of the directors who reported to him. When the affair broke up she alleged sexual harassment. The company made a cursory investigation, decided the senior VP was wrong, and fired him because it had an extremely tough sexual harassment policy. He then filed suit against the corporation for wrongful discharge and defamation of character. His wife has left him and taken their children. What started as a simple affair mutated into trouble for everyone.

Even when legal harassment doesn't result, personal harassment may follow a breakup. Two executives, Carol and Bill, were working well together on a project. Then one day, Carol's boss called her into his office and asked her why Bill said he didn't want to work with her anymore.

"I said, 'Hunh?' " Carol remembered. " 'I just don't understand it.' " She continued, "Imagine this situation. Here I was sitting in my boss's office, and I didn't want to tell him that Bill and I had a one-night stand in Chicago. We were both single, and I didn't think it would hurt. It happened eight months ago. And my boss is saying, 'This person says he doesn't want to work with you anymore, but he's too good a guy to tell me why.' And I thought, 'Oh my God, how do I protect myself?'

"Luckily I was thinking on my feet and I said to my boss, 'Look, you take a poll of everybody in his department and find out if there is anyone there who doesn't want me working with them, and I bet there isn't one.' He did it, came back, and told me I was right. A month later, in fact, he said, 'It must have been his problem because you worked out so well. Everybody likes you.'

"Then a year later I was on a trip with Bill. We were in a bar and I said, 'Would you please explain why you did this to me?' "

" 'I didn't mean any harm,' he said, 'but every time I'd be with you, I'd get horny and start feeling attracted to you, and it was distracting me.' Here's a guy who I thought was a mature man saying, 'I can't work with you in the office because we had a brief fling, broke up, you are still sexually disturbing, therefore I had to get rid of you.' "

A vice president of a corporation of 40,000 people had a different feeling about breakups. "I know a lot of examples where people have had affairs and broken up, but quite honestly it has always worked all right. They've been able to get along on the job.

"There's a period of time when they pull apart, especially if one of them was still in love when they broke up. After a while they become, if not friends, at least acquaintances. So they muddle through the awkward interlude and then can get along."

This is particularly tough for women to do, according to consultant Arleen LaBella. Males have had experience learning to interact with people in situations where what they are doing is more important than with whom they are doing it. "Boys learn that because they need a certain number of players on the team, they have to play with some boys they don't like. Girls growing up didn't usually play team sports, and if they didn't like another girl, they'd just say, 'Let's not play.' "

Breakups are never easy, but on the job they are thornier. If one half the couple is stranded, the pain can be unbearable, and the resulting emotions, however vitriolic, must somehow be held in check with a "the job is bigger than both of us" attitude. Both members have to continue to play the game.

## THE JEALOUS SPOUSE

One of the casualties of corporate romance is the jealous spouse —in most cases so far, the wife. Not only do male and female executives work together in the office, but they now often travel together, a bitter reality for stay-at-home wives to accept. Husbands who work are more likely to be understanding when their wives travel, but they don't necessarily like it either.

An executive told me about a meeting her company had once for sixty sales reps, their spouses, and managers in Florida near Disney World. Late one night, a group of single female employees were sitting in a hot tub with some of the guys who'd been drinking a little too much, and some of the wives were just outraged. They went to the district manager to complain about these women of low moral character. It is interesting to note that they didn't complain about the single men who were there; they complained only about the women.

The woman said that she knew some of the wives quite well,

women who trusted her and told her what was bothering them. One wife had said, "Here I am at home and I don't look that great. I'm real tired of taking care of the kids while my husband's off with this exciting, attractive, stimulating woman."

A wife told a female executive who had recently been divorced and was no longer being invited to the homes of the married male executives, "Well, you have to realize that wives are very nervous about finding out that the woman their husbands travel with is divorced and is now available. You're just like a red flag, and you trigger all kinds of emotions."

A director of human resources said, "A lot of wives really put their foot down and did not want their husbands traveling with women, or even driving home at night with a woman. I'd get all the complaints. The wives would call. They'd scream at me." She used to schedule who went on what projects. She'd put the teams together, matching them according to the needed skills.

"A wife called me once and said, 'I'm sorry, my husband's *not* going because Jane's on that trip.'

" 'You'd better talk to your husband, because that's what he's assigned to do,' I told her."

In another case, a husband called the office and wanted to know exactly where his wife was. She was away on a trip, he had phoned her, and she wasn't in her room. "He screamed at us for not keeping tabs on our people," the manager said. This couple was recently married and the wife was used to being independent and apparently was continuing in that tradition after her marriage. One day the husband stormed into the office. The human resources director told the husband, "Sorry, we are not in the business of worrying about what our employees do after hours." The husband was absolutely irate, the director remembered, "but this woman did her job, and her private life did not affect her performance at all, though heaven knows what she was doing at night.

"I calmed him down for about forty-five minutes. I finally told him he had to handle it at home. When his wife came back to the office she was terribly embarrassed. The story was all over the place. I spent an hour with her," said the director, "and told her she was going to have to go out there in the office and explain to everyone what had happened."

She said, "It's none of their business."

"Okay, tell them that," the director suggested, "but people were concerned for you. They thought after a while, 'Oh my goodness, maybe the guy is right. Maybe something has happened to her.' If you want to avoid further embarrassment, all you have to do is check in at night. It's your responsibility to communicate with your husband, and not let it get to the stage that it did. If it happens again," the director warned, "we're going to wonder what is wrong with your judgment." It never happened again.

In another example of male jealousy, a husband whose wife recently fell in love with the president of a large corporation is so angry with her and the company that in his own business, a key industry in the area, he is boycotting the company's products.

Sometimes, crushed by suspicion and frustration, a spouse will write to the head of a company and complain. In one such case, a woman wrote to the top boss, lamenting that her husband, the father of their several children, was abandoning their twenty-year-old marriage, divorcing her, and going to live with a much younger woman who worked in another part of the corporation. His wife asked, "What kind of behavior are you encouraging? Your company is to blame for the wreck of my marriage. . . ."

Obviously a company cannot take sides on such an issue. If a wife writes this kind of letter, Dr. Macleod suggests that she be told to work it out for herself. Usually the people at the top are in no position to make moral judgments—and have no responsibility—to arbitrate such matters.

In Seattle, Washington, a woman named Veronica Parker tried to hold the corporation responsible in a court of law. She sued the United States Steel Corporation, saying that her former husband,

James, had been transferred to Seattle, leaving her at home in Billings, Montana, with the children. He began an office affair, divorced his wife, and married his lover.

The suit alleged that the "corporate employer knew, or should have known, of the nonmarital relationship, negligently failed to inform Veronica of the relationship, and failed to enforce a company policy of discouraging such relationships."

A lower court dismissed the claim, and the Appeals Court agreed, saying that "United States Steel owed no duty to its employees' spouses to monitor and safeguard their marriages, and therefore could not be held liable. . . ."

The marriages of the Eighties and Nineties, more and more often, with both partners working in a business setting, are going to have to be strong enough to stand the pressure of competition. One might well formulate a proposition stating that the degree of jealousy in a spouse is inversely related to the quality of the marriage. The more jealousy, the less substantial the marriage. Where a marriage is good, working and traveling with other men and women should provide variety, interest, and a lot of stories to share over a glass of wine.

## THE THREAT OF FAVORITISM AND POWER

There has always been favoritism in companies. As one male executive described it, "There are fraternity brothers, people who played football with and against each other, people who golf and sail and play tennis together, drinking buddies, the water-walkers who have all kinds of sponsorship in the organization, the superstars on the fast track."

Male favoritism does exist, but it is simply harder to determine. One doesn't imagine that a man got ahead because he was better-looking, but he well might have, and often does. John Gabarro says male-male favoritism is harder to ferret out because men don't make eyes at each other at the elevator. There may be favoritism because they enjoy the same sports, share common values and attitudes. This may be found in nonsexual relationships where, say, the boss and his woman employee are Harvard Business School graduates. They hit it off because they speak the same language.

"The relationship becomes threatening and disruptive when a direct working connection exists between two people and the constellation of colleagues around them is dependent on one or both," he said.

Professor Gabarro gives the example of a woman in charge of the testing function of a research and development lab. There are four or five project managers, and she provides the scarce resources of testing time and equipment and the people to run the tests and make evaluations. If she fell in love with one of the project managers, questions would be raised among the other managers over whether she would deal with them equitably.

An executive told me about a woman in her office who was sleeping with the president and doing badly at work. "I had no recourse whatsoever. I felt I couldn't complain. Who needs it?" She felt they were getting in the way of her doing her job, and of the success of the project.

She admitted jealousy on her part. "Even though, God knows, I didn't want to get involved with him, there was the feeling of 'How come he likes her more than he likes me?' Women are hit harder by it than men. I think some men like the idea of the workplace as a little stud farm. They think that's cute. I think they still feel the same way, with few exceptions, as they did in the stone age."

People in the office began to tell the woman anything they wanted the president to know. "And damned if it didn't work," the executive remembered.

Sexual favoritism is particularly disrupting because it exposes men's and women's egos. Employees fret, "Is he or she more attractive or younger-looking than I am?" Or, "Why can't I have someone here I care about?" Or, "I have to work hard while they are having fun playing around." Or, "How will it affect us if they break up?" Or, "Why is he getting what I should be getting?"

Perceptions of favoritism can demolish a career. A person could be doing a superlative job, but the evaluation of the work could be damaged if people think she or he is going to bed with the person doing the evaluating.

Do women and men sleep their way to the top? It's been done in fact, fiction, fantasy, and myth. Professor Ellen Berscheid says, "I would suspect using sex to get ahead is much less common than it was before because women are now demanding respect as individuals apart from their sexual and personal qualities, respect as workers in their own right. Now there are an awful lot of women who would say, 'If I ever did anything like that, I'd hate myself.' "

Most executives I conferred with laughed at the idea. Jane Snyder, a director in the division of medical affairs at E. R. Squibb & Sons, said, "You have to have competence to get to the top. Sleeping your way up sounds like you don't need anything but a water bed."

Says Nancy Brown, "If women slept their way to the top with the same frequency that we hear talk of it, there'd be a lot more women at the top. And I question the logic in that myth, because the pattern I have seen over and over again is that the woman who sleeps with someone does *not* get promoted. What happens typically is that the man feels guilty, embarrassed, and wonders if he is being used. He questions his ability to judge her competence. So in an attempt to bend over backwards to be fair, he won't do it. He'll block her advancement."

"I never heard of a woman who slept her way to the top," proclaimed Arthur D. Little's Frederic Withington, "though there are women who have affairs with their co-workers and their customers." I asked him if he'd be upset if a woman used her sex to get some business in a competitive situation.

"Certainly I would," he said. "If I were selling a computer business to someone and the IBM salesperson turned out to be a glamorous woman, and I learned they had an affair prior to his ordering the system, I would darn well be suspicious of sex being a factor. I would probably complain, at least casually, to the people around me.

"But I have always maintained that the importance of such contacts and relationships has usually been minimal in the end. The procurement of a computer system will be done mainly on the facts. The club membership for the man may get you a little more time, or a little more courtesy, but the boss is going to make his decision based on the facts. And, I suspect, even a sexual relationship, while it might be fun, is unlikely to get you anything except extra attention to your sales pitch. The employer is not going to buy something that is a bad deal for him."

A male executive snorted at the question. "Women using sex to get a contract? I'm sure there have been. And men have provided call girls for the evening to get contracts, because they figure that's what the client's going to want."

A male advertising vice president thinks women using sex to get ahead are more the exception than the rule. He said he found most women get promotions because, knowing they go in with one strike against them by just being female, they work harder. He thought a woman using sex to get ahead would no longer be viewed as an intelligent human being. It would muddy up the waters. He admitted that sex is used at times to buy accounts, "but there is nothing sold in today's world without the potential for bribery." He conceded he might send his prettiest salesperson to get an account if he thought it would work. "To win an account, you would do almost anything within your own moral confines. For each of us, that covers a large bit of territory."

Trying to sleep your way to the top can backfire. You might move up for a while but, says Dr. Jennifer Macleod, "the chances that that person will keep moving you up with him are rather remote. People also have heart attacks or change their minds. If he has moved you ahead unfairly, where the hell are you then? With your protector gone, you won't be able to do the job."

Another advertising executive said she was sure some women slept their way to the top, perhaps because they were attracted to power, and were naturally drawn to someone with influence. "It has often been said that women are not good gamesmen, that they don't play the same kind of corporate game as men do. I maintain that women play a different game entirely," she suggested. "There are situations where you have an edge as a woman. And either you decide you are going to be exactly like a man and play the game on his level, or you use whatever you have to get what you want. I'm not suggesting you sleep your way to the top; you just approach people as a woman, rather than as a man. In an all-male environment, it can be very effective for a woman to use that difference."

## TRAVELING WITH THE OPPOSITE SEX

Men and women traveling together present an awkward problem for business people. Is it an automatic signal for the couple to go to bed? How do you get out of such a delicate situation? Wives and husbands may not like their spouses out on the road, but what about the travelers themselves?

The budget director of a large East Coast corporation said she spent a couple of weeks in a motel at a special in-house training course and was the only female with thirty men. There was no problem. They knew her well enough to understand what her attitudes were toward her job and her life. Sometimes, she thought, they seemed to forget she was a woman, which was the way she wanted it.

A banker told me she has traveled with many men over the years and never played around. She would be with the same men all over California and Florida, and "we were always as professional as we could be. Nobody ever made a pass at me." They were always equals or she was the superior officer. Sometimes they would go out and dance, but there was never anything suggestive.

A number of men reported in my interviews with them that they lie to their wives and tell them they are traveling with other men when, in fact, they are with single women. Psychologist Meredith Titus hears a lot from male executives about the stress these situations create at home.

An executive told her recently about getting snowed in in a large city. Because the company executives could not get hotel rooms, they all stayed in a company-owned apartment. There were several men and a woman. When the executive returned home, he spent five days trying to dodge his wife's probing questions. "For the slightly older executives who come from more traditional backgrounds," she said, "and whose wives are in more traditional roles themselves, it can be extremely agitating."

Most men and women, however, seem to be able to handle it professionally by sending out signals indicating their interest in extracurricular activities. Young couples who have always known each other in a professional context understand that travel is part of the job and they trust each other. But if they are looking for the opportunity, it is there.

One vice president remarked, "I've seen people who've been married for some time, and when they get on the road, they think it's a vacation. They think, 'I'm away from home and no one will know what I'm doing.' This is probably more common among men than women. They say sixty percent of men are unfaithful to their wives at some point. Is it fair to say that sixty percent of men on the road fool around?"

## THE CONVENTION CAPER

"Switching rooms happens," said a lawyer, "but I think it's overestimated. I'd be surprised if, in a professional convention where people came from all over the country, it happens more than ten percent of the time."

Dr. Macleod also believes that the degree of sexual activity at conventions is exaggerated. "Men create this myth," she said, "because they don't know any other way to relate to women. They've known them only as mothers, wives, daughters, and sex objects, and nothing else. So if they are on a trip with someone who isn't a wife, daughter, or mother, then clearly she's a sex object. Hotels used to expect it."

When she first started going on business trips with male colleagues, registration clerks assumed that because they had different last names they were checking in for one purpose only. They were usually assigned adjoining rooms with a door between. "It could be very embarrassing," she laughed. "The guy was next door and he could hear you when you took a shower or flushed the toilet." This doesn't happen as much anymore, she said, because of the large number of men and women who are traveling strictly on business.

However, others disagree about convention behavior. One executive commented with a jaundiced eye, "On trips, the conventions are one long pajama party. To me, that really is pretty sleazy. The least they could do is get a nice room at the Plaza on their own. But to use a three-day layover in Kansas City to screw around has always seemed to me pretty low.

"And sales conferences. When I worked for a large corporation in New York, people talked about how, if you stayed up really late or got up really early in the morning and looked out in the hallway —I mean, people were going in and out of rooms all night. It was a joke."

A pharmaceutical executive said, "As much sex goes on at conventions as the males can arrange. Many try to get an assistant they can legally take along. Or you see them maneuvering very early in the meeting toward the attractive young women. It's

'Let's just have a little fun when we're away from home.' That goes on everywhere."

An oil company middle manager recalled, "I've seen men who are different away from home. They are wild, as though they had been unbridled. They are too forward and completely obnoxious. Lots of women are willing to go to bed with them." He said he also knew of women who went to conventions they weren't even associated with. They would pay and go by themselves, just looking for men. Although he claims to have seen a lot of playing around, he said he never saw it among colleagues in the same company.

Another witness to a lot of frantic activity among executives, a male vice president himself, said, "What you see at conventions are guys who don't get out a lot. Once a year they just go nuts and blow it all in a week."

What pressures is the traveling executive reacting to at conventions? Dr. Brian Gould says there are good psychological reasons for bad social behavior at conventions. "It's a vacation from the ordinary rules. That poor guy who drives the speed limit, pays his kid's tuition, buys braces, and listens to his boss, his wife, and his mother-in-law, is out of town for two days, and can get drunk and sleep with someone strange. Often he does it and feels great for having done it. One is always attracted to people one shouldn't be."

An even simpler explanation for bad behavior or the sexual blunders many men make comes from the Management Institute of the University of Wisconsin. In 1980, Dr. Alma Baron, a professor of management, queried 30,000 male managers about their attitudes, and received responses from 8,000 of them. Reacting to the statement "Men do not know how to deal with women executives in social situations," 38 percent agreed. In other words, more than one third of the male executives are apt to make foolish social mistakes because of their confusion over women's new executive roles and, as a result, tumble back into the inappropriate, sexually conditioned responses they grew up on.

## THE PRESSURES OF CORPORATE LOYALTY

Now that men and women executives have friendships, affairs, and marriages with each other, how does that impinge on their corporate loyalty? Corporations worry about secret information being divulged. They worry about conflicts of interest, as in the case of Gina Rulon-Miller and IBM. Where does the loyalty of workers having a relationship lie—to each other, or to the corporation? Problems of trust have existed before, but with the added element of sex, the concern is not only whether company secrets will be passed on when a male employee goes to work for a competitor, or takes company knowledge and sets up his own firm, but whether men and women who love each other will pass secrets with even greater abandon. Is there a corporate honor that transcends even love? Or do amorous bonds take precedence over everything?

The answer, without doubt, depends on the sort of person you are. But it can be a tough decision. And you might bow under one pressure one day and a different one the next. Rhona Ritchie, a twenty-nine-year-old British diplomat who had served as second secretary at the British Embassy in Israel, pleaded guilty to having given her Egyptian diplomat lover the contents of diplomatic cables. Love over country? That's going a bit far. She was given a suspended sentence and called "more foolish than wicked" by an understanding judge. Corporations are not likely to be so soft-hearted.

Wharton's Professor Jerome Katz, a behavioral psychologist, finds this question of loyalties arises in a relationship, for example, if you have to decide whether to accept the posting to a distant city or to stay with your lover. "If you don't take the posting," says Professor Katz, "you are putting your loyalty to the other person ahead of your loyalty to the company. That's a burden employers put on people having a relationship.

"But there's another side of that. At the company level there's a belief in meritocracy, and the best human resource management is color-blind, impersonal, based strictly on merit." So, according to Professor Katz, if you begin to weigh issues that are not directly related to the bottom line, you raise the specter of a conflict of loyalties.

A fairly cynical, or truthful, male senior vice president said, "Most people would try to help out a friend; that's where their loyalty lies. Very few people have real loyalty to the company. They are bought by them. You know that's part of the deal going in. You are getting so much of my life for so many dollars. That's what you are buying, but you are not buying my loyalty. That's normally a two-way street."

I asked a corporate officer who works in the same company as her husband if she could keep a secret from him, and whether she ever did. I also asked whether they might tell each other things to gain more power. She said they handled certain kinds of information that they didn't take home with them. "Sure we keep things secret from each other. Everybody who has been a supervisor has personnel problems which are better kept confidential. I think most people observe this. A supervisor-employee relationship is like a doctor-patient relationship."

She wondered why there was such a crisis over lovers or husbands and wives passing secrets to each other. She said rather pointedly, "Secretaries handle a great deal of confidential information, and we don't worry about them going home and talking to their husbands about it. The chairman of the board doesn't lose sleep over what his secretary knows. That happens all the way up and down the line. It's a matter of establishing the proper relationship with people, and then just observing this rapport."

I was assured that even if her husband knew some big move was on, he wouldn't tell her about it until it was made official. "But it's not always human nature," she conceded. "It's human nature to talk about things. And I can't say that everyone would react as we do."

I asked a bright upper-management woman, "If you knew a secret that would help your husband's career, would you tell him?" "Sure," she answered instantly. "My first allegiance is to my husband, not the company. On the other hand, I do have a strong allegiance to the company. If placed in a situation like that, I would have to make some hard decisions. We haven't been in such a predicament. It's easy for me to say one thing now, but I don't know what I would do. I'd be most likely to remove myself from a situation that would put pressure on our marriage." She said she would probably back out of the project.

It is no doubt true that two men or two women who are not lovers, but who are great friends, might give each other secrets and confidential information, but, says a lawyer, "There is a stronger presumption that you'll give more preference to your lover than your golf buddy."

Kaleel Jamison agrees. "Sexual feelings are very strong, and the possibility of giving information to a husband, wife, or lover is much more likely than to a very, very dear friend."

In the final analysis, perhaps what one is willing to do for a friend, lover, husband, or wife depends on one's personal moral standards and how one perceives the corporation. Is it beneficent, or is it an exploiter? Has the person always been understood, promoted, given good assignments and raises? Or has that individual been underpaid and passed over? Another consideration is whether it would truly hurt the company to pass on the information or whether it is just harmless gossip that could help a lover. The pressures are there, but what to expect is unpredictable. In addition, one must admit that men and women are also capable of degrees of friendship. One cannot assume they will automatically have sex or blab everything they know because sex is involved. There are many people who can, and do, keep sex apart from their private professional conduct even when involved in both with the same person. Observes Janice Eddy, "Pillow talk is an outdated concept."

An insurance executive said she would not give her husband a secret even if she thought it would help him. "That situation has happened to me," she recalled. "You just do not share certain things with your spouse or lover when you reach a certain position. I don't think there's a conflict of interest. You have loyalty to the company that's totally separate from that to your husband, even if you are working for the same company."

She thought many of these problems stemmed from the fact that companies promote people without properly evaluating their judgment and their business ethics. They probably put people in positions they aren't prepared to handle. She also suggests that companies do a poor job of briefing executives to understand the behavioral/ethical qualifications for their jobs. Once more, the corporation will shy away from any discussion of the human requirements and promote solely on the basis of sales receipts and who pulled in the biggest profits.

The corporation would have to admit that the passing of vital information is a concern that did not originate when women in high places began having relationships with men in important jobs. Does the corporation automatically assume that the desire for sex is stronger than the male desire for power and money? Would more secrets be passed between lovers in an affectionate embrace than they would between hard-thinking, ambitious men? It is doubtful.

There have been recent legal suits between Thomas's English Muffins and its employees who went to work for a competitor, taking with them the secret of how to get the nooks and crannies in the muffins; between Hertz and its former president, Joseph V. Vittoria, who became president of Avis; and between Pepsico and

Donald Breen, Jr., the executive who moved to Coca-Cola with Pepsi's latest sales campaign plans in his head. Sex is just one more element in the continuing battle of loyalties.

## SHOULD YOU LEAVE OR SHOULD I?

Suppose a relationship has begun, and the couple thinks it will cause a conflict of interest. How do they decide which one of them will leave?

When Jane Cahill, who worked at IBM for twenty-one years and became vice president of corporate communications and government relations, decided to marry Ralph A. Pfeiffer, Jr., an IBM senior vice president, she felt she should resign. She thought that two married people at the very top level could be uncomfortable. She decided to leave, according to reports, because she felt that while her husband might get a crack at the presidency, she never would.

In such a situation, couples may feel that the junior person should leave, be it man or woman, or the person who might most easily be able to find another job. They might decide the one who has been there a shorter time should leave. Or the one who could commute more easily. Or the one who might like to change careers. Or they might not be able to decide.

A products manager told me about a case where two people were living together. Both were divorced, and they had been dating for a long time. She reported to him, and he began to feel uncomfortable about it.

One day he finally said, "It's time for you to leave. You have to look for another job."

She replied, "Why don't *you* get another job?"

He said, "That's ridiculous. I have a higher-paying job and more seniority. You are newer here."

Neither had any intention of leaving, nor of going to a supervisor for advice. They used to have knock-down, drag-out fights behind their closed office doors. Their feud became so distasteful, they finally broke up.

A top executive told me, "I've never come across a man or woman who faced this problem who, in the next job, failed to consider the issue of romance and its effects in that new workplace. My experience has been that if a woman has had to leave a company because of her romantic entanglements, goes to another company for interviews, and feels that she is going to be looked down upon or treated as a second-class citizen because of her previous relationships, I'll bet you dimes to dollars that we are talking about a woman who will simply turn her back on that organization." Men and women whose recommendations from previous employers may mention the reason for the job switch actively look for a place next time where it is not going to cause concern. They have been through a learning experience.

Whether out of self-interest or real altruism, many corporations are spending time and money to create an atmosphere that is not only healthier physically for their employees but which also defuses a lot of damaging tensions and leads to their better mental health. They are spending as much as $1,000 a day for consultants who help employees confront and solve the pressures of the office, such personal problems as depression, alcohol or drug abuse, or problems with children. They provide individual counseling sessions. Sometimes employees are shipped off to retreats where they take part in awareness sessions to help them better understand their co-workers.

The Chase Manhattan Bank in New York, for example, sends twenty executives each year on a week-long, seventy-mile whitewater rafting trip in Utah or Colorado. The river seminars are run by the Menninger Foundation's Center for Applied Behavioral Sciences.

The purpose is to develop new perspectives on being a manager, to learn to handle executive stress and become more sensitive to others. The river seminars are held three times a year at a cost of $2,600 a person; seminars on land for executives are given twelve times a year at a cost of $2,300 per executive, and the foundation offers a once-a-year superseminar for chief executive officers, presidents, or chief operating officers at a cost of $2,700 per person. That's a lot of money to alleviate stress.

It's even more remarkable, in this context, to realize how little (if any) time and money is being devoted to the growing pressure of office romance.

How men and women handle corporate stress of all kinds has become the subject of much concern. Business schools offer courses in the newly sophisticated studies of organizational behavior and human resource management which examine how we behave in the corporate environment, and how to manage this behavior. They also sponsor crash seminars for executives in many cities on the fine points of good management, such as how to deal with controversy, identify corporate and individual values, and confront "people problems." Traveling workshops crisscross the country offering advice to women on everything from standing up to conflict, to communicating, to working effectively with men. The number of courses, workshops, seminars, management consultants, and pieces of equipment involved in ministering to the pressures of human relationships in the workplace almost adds up to a national business crisis.

Well-run corporations that want higher productivity and greater profits must be concerned about these issues. When they invest in exercise equipment and hire management consultants to dig out and solve the human problems, they are demonstrating their desire to defuse the physical, social, and emotional afflictions that overload their executives. The next and obvious step for them is to capitalize on this desire and to address *all* those pressures, not just the safe, fashionable, or easy ones. More and more frequently those that cry out for attention will include the problems of male-female relationships in the office.

## Chapter 5

# THE MENTOR TRAP

*A* short while ago, the president of a billion-dollar international corporation hired a special assistant. Their mentor-protégé relationship has apparently developed into more than just a business connection. They are living together and openly going to parties together. She is getting a divorce. He already has one.

I was told the story by an angry executive in the company. "The guy earns four hundred to six hundred thousand dollars a year, depending on his bonuses. He certainly could arrange to put her in a consulting business or move her elsewhere in the company so she is not reporting to him. They are the subject of malicious gossip. Employees laugh and poke fun at them and don't take her very seriously.

"She is always given a special assignment, like evaluating a program. It seems as though he's going out of his way to create work for her. The thing that's galling is to get a memo from this woman announcing that [first name of president] and I have decided such and such. It's very unprofessional and unbusinesslike.

"People are saying he must be going through a midlife crisis, or can you really depend on a man who is so shortsighted that he doesn't see what he's doing? The women in the company are upset because she's giving women a bad name. Work, though, has not been seriously disrupted because in a big corporation like ours with ten thousand employees you don't see the corporation president every day. You could go eight months and never see the guy.

But what the president is doing makes it harder on other people who are trying to do it the right way."

When not handled properly, the mentor relationship dissolves into crude favoritism and causes reverberations of discontent throughout the entire corporation. It can also impede the work of the company at the top level. The following example was recounted by an executive vice president.

The chairman of the board of a rather large corporation had taken a fancy to a woman and made her his assistant. She sat in on board meetings, for which she obviously was not qualified, and in the eyes of the other executives, she was a spy.

"Whenever you have a small meeting of five or six people, and there is one person who is not by background on an equal footing with the rest of the people, it just creates problems," the vice president said, "especially if this person attempts to participate. Knowing there is a direct conduit back to the chairman of the board obviously changes what people say. That is disruptive, because people aren't saying and doing what they would under normal circumstances. That's not the way to run a business."

When real love develops, it will not invariably cause business problems if properly acknowledged and dealt with. Helen, a young executive, worked for a small company where everyone was very close. She was twenty-seven and had been married for five years. Shawn, her mentor/boss, was thirty-four, had been married for nine years, and had children. She admired him greatly and always thought he was attractive, but had no idea whether or not he was drawn to her. The situation seemed impossible because they were both married. They spent a lot of time together, went on business trips, had lunches, but everything was kept on the boss-subordinate level. "I'm really a very old-fashioned girl," Helen told me, "I don't go around stealing other people's husbands. I've always been monogamous."

One day they went to a company going-away party, and had far too much to drink. As they were leaving the restaurant,

Shawn mentioned that he was going off on a business trip and needed a ride to the airport. She had a car and offered to drive him. It was during that ride that he told her, "We can't go on like this. I'm crazy about you." Then he went away for two weeks. He came back, and four days later she left her husband, he left his wife, and they started living together. Neither of them, she said, had really been in love with their spouses. "If he hadn't said something first," Helen said with a laugh, "we'd still be sitting there."

Shawn handled it by inviting everyone in her department to lunch and telling them they were living together. After the announcement, there was stunned silence, and then some applause. Finally the subject was changed. But he did say she was planning to leave the company. How did people react once the news had settled and everyone was back at work in the office?

"It's important to remember that this company was like a family. We were all-for-one and one-for-all, so it would be inhuman for people not to feel a little put out that one of the kids got to go live with Daddy." They married, she found another job, and he still acts as her mentor in the confines of their living room.

## WHAT IS A MENTOR?

In Greek mythology, Mentor was Odysseus's wise and trusted counselor. In the Middle Ages there were mentors or masters in the various trade guilds, and those who worked with and learned from them were apprentices. A mentor in those days, points out Dr. James Clawson, a professor of organizational behavior at the University of Virginia's Colgate Darden Graduate School of Business Administration, was a powerful person. Legally and morally, he was responsible for his apprentices in terms of behavior in the community and in church, and their social skills in handling clients and doing their trade. "A true mentor," says Professor Clawson, "would be someone I would emulate professionally, financially, socially, politically, in community involvement, perhaps even physically in terms of recreation."

But, he explains, we don't have mentors in the classical sense anymore. People develop in many ways, influenced by the mass media, books, travel, and a wide range of educational experiences. He sees today's mentors as sponsors that people seek, not so much so they can learn, but so that they can be certain of moving up.

In recent years, men and especially women have been goaded by the popular press into looking for a mentor. The importance of having such a senior person in one's life has been dramatized as the sure way, perhaps the only sure way, of receiving the coveted promotions and eventually some of the power. The magazines talk of this mentor as being "your own personal management consultant, an ally, a trusted friend or critic, a support system, a mutual admiration society, a source of good honest feedback." Readers are told it is wise to have an "intimate" friend in high places who will boost their careers. An artificial frenzy has been created in the lower managerial ranks, and, no doubt, women who have been unable to become protégés must wonder what is wrong with them.

The 1979 Korn/Ferry study of senior-level executive men from Fortune 500 companies and their 1982 study of women senior executives found that while only 16 percent of the men felt the "who you know, not what you know" theory of advancement was still valid, as many as 42 percent of the women believed it was true, indicating they feel the importance of a mentor much more keenly. Among the 300 senior-level female executives from the largest U.S. companies, 67 percent of the women said they had a male mentor.

Nevertheless, according to Kathy Kram, professor of organizational behavior at Boston University's School of Management, there are not as many male-female mentor relationships as there are with two men because of the concern over the possibility of intimacy and sexuality. But they do exist and are becoming more common as more women become part of the professional and managerial work force.

"There are no statistics," says Professor Kram, "but from the interviewing I've done, I'd say sexual attraction is quite a common occurrence." She points out that underlying all of these relationships is a mutual respect, admiration, and increasing intimacy, "so the natural fallout of that would be sexual attraction as well, unless there is an extremely wide age difference, in which case it doesn't become an issue."

The mentor-protégé connection is the key to an organization's developmental activities, and to its future. It is a kind of built-in favoritism which is condoned by, and nurtures, the hierarchy, and is accepted with few rumblings by the office. No doubt the fastest way to learn the ropes of corporate life, it is reminiscent of the parent-child dependency, at least in the beginning, where the older person teaches, guides, and helps the younger one to learn, grow, and succeed. Being a mentor is satisfying and stimulating for the older executive, giving him or her a sense of being needed, a new purpose in life, and a new outlet for creative energies in a job which may already have been mastered and become routine. The relationship could end if the older person feels threatened by the younger one's success, especially if the younger one is going to outdo the teacher. Usually there is pride in the discovery of a young talent and helping it mature.

Mentor-protégé unions have received a lot of bad press lately because of the reports of romance and sex which can result, and apparently have, but the importance to the corporation of this informal learning-teaching system remains vital. A business must have intelligent, experienced, worldly managers to solve current problems and guide it to a healthy future. Competent and effective managers must either be developed within the company or brought in from another company where they have gone through the same learning experience.

Therefore, the mentor-protégé system—even with its problems

—may be far more important to corporate survival than has yet been acknowledged. Despite its significance to the corporation, the system is left to chance and exists randomly.

Many executives, however, have commented on the need for these company-sponsored relationships. One advertising senior VP, for example, said that mentors were frequently found in his business because much of what one needs to know comes from experience. "Creative talent is something that has to be molded to fit within guidelines. You can't have a lot of creative people just doing what they want. It would be anarchy. Those who have been around for a long time are able to train and teach others how to adapt their talents to the work we're in."

Given the importance of mentors, it is remarkable that most people don't know how to manage such relationships. This is of particular concern now that there are a growing number of young female executives who must attract the attention of older male executives who are willing to be their mentors. Also, more women in senior positions are becoming mentors to junior men, a situation in which people have even less experience. One problem lies with the fact that there are many similarities between a growing mentor relationship and the evolution of a romantic, intimate relationship. At some point the teaching rapport can suddenly collapse as a man and woman become romantically involved.

Professors Clawson and Kram have charted the course of such mentor-protégé romances. The desire for a liaison can begin when a subordinate develops respect for a superior's expertise which leads to a heightened desire to be closer. The subordinate senses and trusts the superior's general concern for his or her well-being, and this trust reduces the tension so it is easier for the subordinate to approach the boss. As the relationship starts to grow, an informality takes over. The mentor shares information and personal experience with the protégé and describes the subtle mysteries of the job and its pressures.

Professor Kram did a study of eighteen such relationships in a large Northeastern public utility and found that they went through four predictable, but not always distinct, phases:

- In the **initiation** phase, which lasts six to twelve months, both people involved have fantasies about each other. The young manager begins to feel supported and respected by a senior manager who is admired.
- In the **cultivation** phase, which lasts two to five years, the interpersonal bond strengthens, and counseling and friendship develop. The younger person gives the senior technical and psychological support, while the senior feels great satisfaction at being able to express himself or herself through a new generation of managers. The emotional bond deepens.
- In the third phase the young manager may feel stifled, wishes to become independent, and a **separation** takes place that can involve anger and a fight, but certainly includes feelings of loss and anxiety. He misses having her around. She misses his support.
- In the last phase, there is a **redefinition** of the friendship, the stress of separation diminishes, and gratitude and appreciation increase.

If sexual attraction is going to burst forth with intensity, it will happen, I would guess, somewhere in the second phase.

## THE NEW MENTOR ANXIETIES

Professor Kram says she has noticed a reluctance on the part of males to be mentors to women. They are concerned about how others will view the relationship and are afraid that there will be rumors that they are having an affair. Men also find it awkward to initiate informal contact with female employees, fearing that the women will misinterpret it as flirtation. Concern about being charged with sexual harassment is putting a damper on many a man's willingness to be a mentor to a rising young woman. It is hardly worth risking his own career to make this gesture.

In addition, even when a connection is established, the mentor will have to inhibit his or her normal behavior toward a protégé. It is difficult for a male to spend time coaching and counseling a female over drinks and dinner, engaging in the traditional one-on-one informal exchange of information and advice, without rumors starting. The mentor may also refrain from this often valuable after-hours coaching to avoid any possibility of becoming attracted to a young subordinate. These little-understood anxieties will limit the opportunities of rising young stars, and frequently may stunt or even abort a valuable alliance. Thus the corporation can be the loser if the would-be mentor finds the situation too fraught with pitfalls and backs away.

Finding a mentor also encourages a certain amount of peer resentment. The protégé, too, may feel guilt and conflict if he or she is compelled to make a choice between keeping friends and colleagues or continuing an association with the boss despite their jealousy. There are strong competitive dynamics at work among peers who all are trying to advance. If a woman stands out as the one who has an inside track because she is coached regularly by a male, people will assume sex is part of the picture. Otherwise they would have to admit that she is better qualified than they, or smarter. Blaming it on sex is much easier.

During the mentor process, one or the other of the pair may want to extend the boundaries of the relationship to include sex. There are two alternatives in this situation. One is to talk about it openly and discuss the benefits or liabilities of the liaison. The other choice is not to talk about it at all but to decide where the boundaries must be. To refuse the affair may destroy a formerly strong friendship, and either working together will become uncomfortable or the mentor may lose interest in the young person's career.

If the affair proceeds, the young female manager may depend on the mentor for advice to such an extent that, as Professor Kram points out, she will enact the stereotypical role of the dependent one, while he becomes the dominant protector. In such a situation, the woman is afraid to demonstrate her skills and her performance declines.

Dr. Brian Gould, the San Francisco psychiatrist, identifies another new stress that is common when executive women adopt senior men as their mentors. The "mentor" may be a case of "sexual sublimination rather than a true colleagial relationship. When a woman is attractive, she finds herself with many offers of 'professional friendship' that turn out to be the same old sexual game in a new setting—the boardroom instead of the bar."

In the reverse situation, when a woman occupies the senior position in the mentor relationship and a younger man is the junior, Professor Kram says the situation can be difficult and awkward precisely because "there are no stereotypical assumptions and behaviors to rely on." There are more and more cases on record of situations where female bosses have demanded sexual favors from male subordinates. "These are things we thought were historically part of the male role," Professor Clawson points out. Now that the new stereotypical responses are turned upside down, sexual harassment should be associated with the managerial role and no longer thought of as a male prerogative. "Women in the same power positions as men are not immune to the same kinds of sexually inappropriate behavior on the job," notes Professor Clawson. Men and women are discovering a wider range of possibilities than the stereotypes dictate.

Other situations exist that can be extremely frustrating. A financial services corporation executive said she found it difficult to find a mentor because her job involved a lot of traveling and a lot of men had wives and felt it was too difficult to explain what they were doing on the road with a twenty-three-year-old woman. "It was easier *not* to teach me what I needed to know so they didn't have to get involved with me—even though I was married, too."

During this unstable transition stage, the mentor and protégé are subject to a number of push-pull stresses. There is the push to get the relationship working and functioning well for the individuals and the corporation. And there is the pull away from all the tensions and complications which the relationship is currently engendering.

An example of the complexities that arise is the case of the president of a good-sized pharmaceutical company who was the mentor of the female information manager in their medical department. His sponsorship developed into an affair, and her career grew so rapidly as a result that she got her own sales force, which she was not qualified to handle. This went on for two or three years.

Employees made snide remarks about her ability and the fact that the position she held was basically created for her, telltale evidence that sexual favoritism was hard at work. One disgruntled observer remarked, "People's careers were changed because of the affair. Other people did not get jobs they should have gotten because this gal got them."

By allowing a romance to happen, the mentor takes unfair advantage of the protégé, who may easily become infatuated with the glow of power and influence. The mentor bears a special responsibility to guard against the protégé's vulnerability, and make an effort to avoid such folly. This is not to say True Love may not happily and legitimately occur. But mentors need to be especially sensitive to the risks. In time they will develop codes of behavior somewhat like the doctor-patient, lawyer-client, or teacher-student relationships. These also are instances where power can be exploited, but there are ethical standards which have become accepted and which in most, though not all, cases prevent such exploitation.

Professors Clawson and Kram point out that in cases of affairs, colleagues worry about the mentor's judgment and assume that he or she most likely will favor the protégé over all others regardless of the merits of other employees.

Acts of favoritism, they say, whether real or imagined, can demoralize the work force and "dissolve respect and loyalty for you as a leader and manager." When people believe the boss's judgment is compromised, he or she can no longer be an effective manager. Even more unfortunate, the knowledge of this kind of sexual liaison confirms many high-level male biases against women in management, and gives support to the attitude that no special effort should be made to help them. The big risk in this tainted relationship is that the subordinate or even the mentor may be passed over for a promotion, or even fired.

On the other hand, if the mentor remains aloof, the danger exists that not only will the whole dynamic behind the process lose its force and vitality, but the mentor, say Professors Clawson and Kram, will be seen as cold, people will hesitate to approach him regularly and informally, the grapevine will avoid him, and important issues will not be communicated. The male mentor will be perceived as someone who doesn't like having women around, who cannot foster the development of his subordinates. He will end by having a reputation "for being a strict manager who is able to make tough decisions, but one who has not prepared anyone for future leadership of the organization."

## TURNING THE MENTOR ATTRACTION OFF

I spoke to Stan, a boss at a large manufacturing company who was sexually attracted to a female subordinate, and she to him. This was fueled by the fact that they worked closely together on a project. They were both married, but enjoyed the sexual vibrations each felt so that, as someone said, they began to go through what appeared to be a mating dance in diminishing circles. The subordinate urged her mentor to have the affair because she had an open marriage and could handle it. Stan was tempted, but finally decided not to acquiesce. I asked him how he was able to make that decision while he continued to be a mentor who found his subordinate sexually desirable.

He told me that he had sat down and dissected the situation. He told himself that he was seeing only a certain portion of this woman's life. He forced himself to think about and find out about other portions of her life to see whether or not their interests meshed. What kind of food does she like? Does she like to exercise? Do we like similar kinds of music? Do we have enough shared interests? "And when I looked at all the dimensions," he admitted, "I had to confess that my wife and I had more in common than I did with my subordinate."

I asked him how he could have turned his attraction off if this had not been the case. He said he then would have had to ask himself if the commitment he had made to his marriage and his children was more important than pursuing a new relationship, with all its uncertainties. He did, in fact, decide to repress his sexual desires for the sake of everyone concerned. "That was a mental, not an emotional decision," he said. He squelched it by mentally focusing on their differences, rather than their magnetism.

One executive told me that she once had a mentor whom she liked enormously, but she wasn't prepared to pay the price having an affair would have entailed. The price, she thought, would have been the suspicion that her advancement was only because of her interaction with this person. "I didn't want to feel that way about myself," she said.

## THE WOMAN MENTOR

The new phenomenon of the woman as mentor in business has become more common as women reach middle-management status. In the 1982 Korn/Ferry Study of 300 senior women executives in the largest U.S. companies, 67 percent said they were mentors to lower-level men and 78 percent that they were mentors to lower-level women. These are the top women in the top corporations. What the situation is nationally is less clear.

Many women have been accused of being of greater help to women than men. On the other hand, others who have made it to the executive level are said to be reluctant to devote the time, energy, and commitment to being a mentor because they are so busy fighting for what they've accomplished and promoting their own futures. Professor Kram said, "My hunch is that it is so stressful for women to survive in upper levels of management that it may be hard for them to make a lot of energy available to young people."

Looking at the other end of the experience, Professor Kram found it was difficult for young women to accept other women as mentors. "When I work with students, the closer we are in age, the more difficult it is for them to see me as a genuine authority because they have been socialized to view men, rather than women, as experts in a professional context, so they discount the woman's value. Second, because women are more willing to accept the power differential with men than they are with women, they may find fault with them rather than wanting to learn from them." If this sounds as if we're suffering from cultural lag because we still adhere to such outdated notions, it is because we are. In the same way that most women will choose male doctors, they find it difficult to view other women as people with expertise. In a *Wall Street Journal*/Gallup Organization survey done in October 1984 of 722 female executives having the title of vice president or higher, 29 percent said they would rather work for a man, while only 4 percent preferred to work for another woman.

One of the reasons for this, believes consultant Arleen LaBella, is that women have been socialized to relate to each other as rivals. "Since we were young, most women have been raised to think the best we could do for ourselves would be to land a successful man, and that we are in competition with every other woman in the world to find that man. So from the early years on, we think of other women not as our collaborators but as our competitors." However, she believes that as they gain experience in business, women will learn that empowering one another empowers themselves.

For the most part, however, problems persist. A young woman from one of New York's top banks told me she has a "negative mentor" who is very jealous of her because she knows a lot, while the older woman apparently got where she is more through luck and personality—exposing her full bosom in low-cut blouses, flirtation, and a knowledge of sports—than with skill. "She is not confident of her ability and is afraid I might point out to her what she doesn't know." Her mentor is also envious of the young woman's marriage to an executive in the same bank, and has actually held her subordinate back by refusing to allow her to travel, as bank policy indicates she should, or to attend lunches for her clients.

Says this young executive, "If another woman is having a hard time, women can be sympathetic and supportive. But if a woman is getting ahead and doing well, a lot of women have trouble being really happy for her. I think the Queen Bee syndrome—women not wanting to see other women succeed—is very much alive." Nevertheless, there are a lot of successful women, as Korn/Ferry documented, who are eager and willing to help young women.

If you are a man, having a woman mentor has its own stresses. Said one young executive, "If I'm a male subordinate and I have a female boss, and she starts trying to coach me, I will try to sort out, maybe consciously or even subconsciously, how much of what she does is sex related, and how much of what she does is managerial. In this transitional period, people are going to be wrestling with that."

## WHEN TO LOOK FOR YOUR MENTOR

Obviously, the junior person is helped in important ways by the advice and encouragement of a senior member of the organization. In fact, the mentor system is one that can support people at many stages of their careers, helping them to understand what they should be thinking about and planning next and to make the right decisions in areas of professional choices, and teaching them the subtleties of business politics.

Should one set out immediately after settling into a new job to search for a kindly soul to call one's mentor? Perhaps, if that person is to take on the teaching role. But a mentor who is to be a sponsor for the younger person can only help someone who can contribute independently to the workings of the corporation, who has achieved a recognized expertise and is not likely to encounter things he or she can't handle. This middle-career stage is the time to have a champion at one's side, "to advance my cause in those inner-circle meetings I'm not privy to," as Professor Clawson puts it. You want someone in the inner circle who will say, "Hey, So-and-So is hot stuff. You really ought to promote her."

He also mentions the advantages of an alternative to the mentor—the group mentor. He suggests that the person could feed his or her ideas to people in the inner circle, work on committees with several of them, and channel reports through several members of the inner circle, so when the top executives meet together, "I don't have one sponsor, but I have a group of partial sponsors." The benefits of this situation could be just as effective as having a single mentor. It would also protect the junior from the dangers of attrition. If a job change or illness forced one's mentor to leave, there would always be others who knew one's work.

## TIPS FOR MENTORS, PROTÉGÉS, AND <u>CORPORATIONS</u>

Professors Clawson and Kram, as well as a number of executives, have provided specific advice on how to avoid setting the stage for sexual attraction. Every situation is different, but these tips are offered as a distillation from which you can draw your own conclusions.

- Women protégés should be more assertive and self-confident and less automatically deferential to authority so they are seen as people, rather than in the stereotypical role of the female. This assertiveness should be informed and intelligent, not brash and pushy.
- Men and women in a mentor-protégé relationship who feel themselves becoming attracted might assume a father-daughter stance to ward off any consideration of sexual involvement. It can be temporary, but will enable the pair to work together more easily.
- If you copy a father-daughter dynamic, the woman should not fall into a stereotype which keeps her deferential. Daughters can be aggressive and independent, too.
- To find the best mix of friendliness and objectivity toward their female protégés, male managers should confer and share experience about what to do and what not to do, rather than tackling awkward problems alone in the dark.
- If a mentor falls in love with a protégé, a new mentor should be found to take over the teaching job.
- Both people should try to define their emotional boundaries. If the relationship crosses that boundary, the two should consider not acting on their mutual attraction and maintaining a professional relationship.
- In case of sexual attraction, the mentor should consider

the negative impact of the romance on the subordinate's career.

- Examine all aspects of the person to see whether the sexual attraction is superficial.
- Use first names, but don't use pet names or nicknames.
- Avoid meeting alone after hours too often or for too long.
- Leave your office door open during meetings.
- Include others if you have to meet alone after hours or during times of stress and deadlines.
- Don't discuss personal or family subjects and don't give personal advice.
- Be sure to take all your subordinates to lunch so no one person is perceived as being favored.
- Make your protégé's skills known to others. Invite senior managers and subordinates to meet with you, even if there is no direct need. This will defuse suspicions if you promote her or him.
- Distribute copies of work the subordinate has done and ask for comments.
- Don't promote the protégé until enough time has gone by for others to be convinced she or he is worthy.
- Use the same language and tone of voice with the protégé as you do with others—no inside jokes to indicate something special is going on.
- Have many contacts and support systems in the organization to avoid the suspicion that your relationship with any one person is sexual.
- If you decide to go ahead and have the romance, make sure it will enrich, and not diminish, your self-worth, that your mentor is not exploiting you, that his or her interest is not just sexual, that there is a real emotional commitment. Or, if you both agree it is sex and just that, then keep it that way to avoid complications.

- Know your values. If you are married, do you want to get sexually involved with a mentor? How do you feel about being unfaithful to your spouse? If you are clear about what you will and won't do, you will avoid predicaments. Anticipate them *before* you find yourself in the middle of them.
- Find mentors by having a number of relationships up, down, and across the organization. Establish long-term contacts by attending the right meetings and getting on committees that involve people who are potential mentors. Circulate your ideas and results to these people, and arrange luncheons and discussions.
- Be flexible enough to respond to your mentor's needs. Be dependable, even if it means changing your vacation time or rescheduling a weekend away. Though mentors should not demand or expect their protégés to be on twenty-four-hour call, crises do come up.
- Corporations should establish reward systems and educational programs that encourage executives to improve the quality of their male-female relationships, and to develop an interest in mentoring.
- Make the mentor role part of most executives' jobs so that they are held accountable in their performance reviews for these developmental activities. Make it clear that unless they are grooming managers for the future, they are going to inhibit their own promotion and advancement.

## DO MENTORS HAVE A FUTURE?

Executive recruiters estimate that it takes fifteen to twenty-five years to become a top executive. That means it will take about twenty years before the next generation, presumably a more sexually relaxed one, is in a position to set the tone for a natural attitude toward the mentor relationship. In the meantime, there will no doubt be more cases of mentors mismanaging situations they find uncomfortable to deal with, as well as more gossip, more suspicion, and more accusations and perceptions of affairs where none exist. It seems to me, though, that to bow to these pressures just because someone in the office enjoys gossip is to hurt the corporation, the mentor system, and the individuals.

As one executive said, "We are going through an awkward period. It feels like adolescence for organizations and people. We're learning how to handle something new and it's difficult. So we are 'klutzes' at it sometimes."

Young people coming into organizations today have had more experience relating to each other, living with each other, working together as nothing more than best friends, and they will function more easily with the other sex without getting nervous and flustered. They won't be tense over the prospect of being a mentor, and their subordinates will understand what it's all about. This doesn't mean that they won't ever fall in love, but it also doesn't mean that working together will create as much sexual stress or that those who see couples working together will automatically assume a sexual motive.

Although tomorrow's managers will have had a different kind of socialization than today's have had, if some organizations continue to force them and their younger subordinates into an antiquated mold and try to make them conform to today's worst narrow-minded standards, heavy with sexual clichés, problems will persist. For the corporation to get the most out of its young people and out of the mentor system, there will have to be organization-wide changes in attitude.

A growing number of companies have begun to realize that in order to provide managers for the future, they have to make more efficient use of the current elite mentor system, rather than leave it to whim and hope their senior managers will want to teach their young people the secrets of the corporate world.

They have therefore democratized the system and prescribed a plan whereby a group of senior managers is chosen and asked to act as mentors to a group of junior people in the company. Men and women are assigned to each other randomly. Unfortunately, they aren't prepared to be mentors; they are merely told that this is their role.

Such hesitant efforts have had mixed results in the financial institutions and food-products firms that have tried them. Professor Clawson reports that some people said they didn't like their mentors; others didn't like their protégés. They had little in common, were too busy, or learned too little.

The idea, however, is intriguing. Why not institutionalize a proper mentor system and break down stereotypes so that corporations don't wait twenty years for male-female office behavior to change? Senior and junior people who are about to enter a mentor program should be taught the value of the system, what is in it for them and for the corporation, and how to manage unexpected sexual attractions. The money spent on this program would be comparatively small and very worthwhile. After all, what is more important to a corporation than the quality of its managers?

The corporation, says Professor Clawson, if it's wise, should create a nurturing, receptive environment which fosters the growth of an informal mentor-protégé system. "In other words, if you have a fertile garden, you throw the seeds out, and you let them grow. But some corporate cultures are like pavement. You throw the seeds out, they bounce off and are washed away by the first rain."

## THE BILL AND MARY SHOW

It would be hard to guess how many tons of newspaper copy have been churned out describing the woes of Bill Agee and his wife, Mary Cunningham, the most celebrated mentor-protégé pair in the annals of business. Their example, as everyone has heard, is a classic case of the mismanagement of a boss-subordinate corporate romance. Given their intelligence and capabilities, it seems incredible that they so mishandled their situation. One can only presume that although successful in business, Agee had no experience handling a romance or friendship at work, and neither did Cunningham. They made every possible mistake. To demonstrate what I mean, imagine yourself as Cunningham-the-protégé taking this quiz:

**Answer the following questions by checking Yes or No.**

YES  NO

- ☐  ☐  Should you have a drink with your boss alone in his office every evening after work?
- ☐  ☐  Should you give press interviews on your relationship if you want to stay discreet?
- ☐  ☐  Should you attend political conventions and tennis matches and be photographed sitting side by side?
- ☐  ☐  Should you rent apartments across the hall from each other?
- ☐  ☐  Should you report only to the man with whom gossip says you are having an affair?
- ☐  ☐  Should you flaunt the fact that you have the ear of your boss and are his primary advisor?
- ☐  ☐  Should you take two-bedroom suites in hotels when traveling together on company business?
- ☐  ☐  Should you often make comments like, "Bill and I were talking . . . ," reminding your colleagues of the fact that you have a privileged relationship with the boss?
- ☐  ☐  Should you be seen in public holding hands?
- ☐  ☐  Should you tell people at work that the boss came home early from his vacation to take you to a rock concert?

Mary Cunningham would have had to answer yes to every question, because in fact she did all those things. She rationalized bad business behavior by insisting she did not want to give in to rumor and antifemale stereotypes. Any competent business executive, either male or female, would probably not have answered yes to a single question. All one needs is common sense to get a perfect grade.

The history of "The Bill and Mary Show" (as it has been called), if anyone has missed it, is as follows. William Agee, the forty-four-year-old chief executive of the billion-dollar Bendix Corporation, hired an executive assistant, Mary Cunningham, fresh out of Harvard Business School, his alma mater. Cunningham joined Bendix in June 1979. A year later, in June 1980, Agee promoted her to vice president for corporate and public affairs. In September, he appointed her vice president for strategic planning. She resigned under pressure in October. Agee and she were both divorced from their spouses during this period and married in June 1982.

Agee's own career climb had been swift. He went from Boise Cascade to Bendix's top job in eleven years. Cunningham became a top vice president and the chief's main advisor in a mere fifteen months. The protégé was beginning to usurp the mentor's position, or so it seemed. Agee announced to his colleagues that Cunningham had "been my right and left arm ever since she came into the company. She is the most vital and important person within the company and has played an important part in conceptualizing the strategy." Cunningham called herself his "alter ego" and "most trusted confidante," and "best friend." The corporation officers began to worry about who was running the place. Cunningham was accused of sleeping her way to the top, and Agee was thought to be guilty of favoritism. Both insisted they were not having an affair, despite Cunningham's incredible lack of discretion (see quiz above).

In fact, Cunningham answered such perceptions by comparing

herself to her mother, who raised her while living with a Catholic monsignor, Father William Nolan, curate of the local church. Her boss at Bendix had the same first name, and Cunningham says her relationship with Agee was like the one her mother had with that other Bill, "another Platonic relationship the world didn't understand."

Cunningham's life and career were hardly average. During her senior year at Wellesley she met Howard R. Gray, Jr., a black man eleven years her senior who was attending Harvard Business School. They married within a year. After graduation, she worked as a paralegal, then as a junior officer at Chase Manhattan Bank for three years. She entered Harvard Business School in 1977, and a week after graduation was hired at Bendix.

Is Cunningham being unfairly maligned by all the people who think she used sex to get ahead and wasn't nearly as smart as Agee thought she was? Or as *Fortune* magazine asked, "Is any twenty-nine-year-old fresh from business school, no matter how smart, qualified to be the chief planning executive of a multibillion-dollar corporation in the throes of a major reconstruction?" What sort of person was she?

In *Three Plus One Equals Billions: The Bendix–Martin Marietta War,* author Allen Sloan reports after extensive interviews with people who knew Cunningham over the years, and some who worked closely with her at Bendix, that "there is an almost unanimous portrait of a person lacking in both practical business experience and emotional maturity." She is described by Sloan's observers as someone who had a lot of energy, was not an original thinker, who "would take other people's ideas and make them her own, a flatterer, a woman who was bright and quick, very good with business jargon, but who had considerable difficulty in making decisions."

Sloan says Cunningham enjoyed throwing her power around at Bendix, and would schedule meetings for weekends or during people's vacations so they would have to return at her bidding.

She made it known to the assembled group one day at Agee's house that she knew exactly where the phone was in Agee's bedroom.

After being forced to resign from Bendix, she supposedly received a hundred offers of employment, which, say those who follow such stories, were a result of Agee's string-pulling. She joined Seagram, tried to divide her time between working there and plotting strategies for Agee during the Bendix-Marietta takeover fight, was said to be unpopular at Seagram, and finally left to become head of the company she formed with Agee, a venture capital and strategic consulting firm called Semper, jokingly known on Wall Street as "Whimper."

Not content to let the tumult die a natural death, Cunningham wrote a book, *Powerplay: What Really Happened at Bendix*, published in 1984. In it, she went to great lengths to describe her prudish Catholic girlhood and shyness with boys. She noted that Agee's marriage was a failure and that neither his wife nor Bendix's top executives understood him. She comes out looking like Saint Mary, the only one who can save Bendix, something she will do because she wants so much to help people, even though it is an exhausting job. She wrote constantly about "strategy" as though, as one reviewer quipped, "it is some ability of excellence known only to her." *Fortune* referred to her as "an almost clinical egomaniac," "an audacious phony," and called her habit of dropping business-school buzzwords "infantile." If there is a business thought in Cunningham's head it doesn't emerge in the book, and critics called her "boring and whiny."

Why did she write a 286-page explanation, feeding the scandal she should have put behind her? Was it to set the record straight? Was it to put down on paper what she wants the world to believe about her? Or was it to expurgate any guilt she may feel from having disrupted a lot of people's lives? She seems, more than anything, to be trying to justify her own life.

Despite the elaborate apologia put together by Mary Cunningham, the book's message was unfortunately marred by a Freudian slip or an embarrassing typographical error. " . . . This isn't a crime I want people to forget. There's a lesson—lessons —in this entire experience that ought to be made clear. Sexual accusations are serious ones. They can ruin personal lives and they can ruin careers. And with more and more women rising up the corporate leader [sic], the weapon of sexual accusations will be used again."

In the meantime, as one tries to unfold all the angles of this corporate soap opera, it is obvious that Agee's mismanagement of his role as mentor wiped out the esteem he had built. Expressing interest in bidding for RCA, he was informed, in the now-famous quote, that he hadn't even "demonstrated his ability to manage his own affairs, let alone someone else's," and he withdrew. After Bendix failed to acquire Marietta, but was taken over by Allied Corporation, it became clear that Agee would never be chief operating officer of Allied, and he resigned.

He lost his marriage, he left his job, he was not named Transportation Secretary (an appointment he reportedly lobbied for), and *Newsweek* quoted a top executive of a Fortune 500 firm as saying, "There is no place for Bill Agee in American business [any time soon]." This is one mentor who made a mess of the relationship. If you wonder how it all happened, and you are a male and a mentor or a potential one, then take the following quiz:

**Check Yes or No before the statements below, to indicate whether or not you would:**

YES   NO
☐      ☐   Hire a bright MBA right out of college and make her your protégé; one year later, make her a vice president.
☐      ☐   Have her report personally to you so that no one else can really assess her work and judge its quality.

147

# CORPORATE ROMANCE

☐ ☐ When rumor has it that a number of executives have complained about your relationship with your protégé, fire the key man before he can take the matter to the Board of Directors.

☐ ☐ Ignore criticism that your protégé has undue influence over you and company policy.

☐ ☐ Three months after making your bright protégé a vice president, elevate her to an even more important position where she and you alone plot corporate strategy.

☐ ☐ Respond to criticism and growing unrest among corporation officers by discussing it publicly, and telling a meeting of 600 employees that your protégé is only a close friend, a close friend of the family's, and her rapid promotions have been justified. Announce that you are not sleeping with her.

☐ ☐ Invite *Fortune* magazine to have free run of the corporation to do a story on you and your protégé and dispel rumors about your affair.

☐ ☐ When your alleged romance becomes national news, tell the press you will make a joint announcement, thus sparking interest—then cancel it.

☐ ☐ Attend public occasions such as the U.S. Open tennis matches and the Republican National Convention with your protégé instead of your wife. Be sure to hold hands.

☐ ☐ Divorce your wife of twenty-three years and marry your protégé, putting rumors about your affair to rest once and for all.

☐ ☐ To instill confidence in your professionalism during a crucial business crisis, pose in a

148

photograph for *People* magazine on your knees
in front of your protégé, now your new wife.

☐   ☐   During critical, sensitive meetings with another
corporation in a takeover battle, instead of
bringing experienced officers of your
corporation to advise you, take only your wife.
Assume that a young woman only several years
out of business school would give you better
counsel than officers with years of experience in
the company.

☐   ☐   If you have not told the truth or find yourself
in a sticky situation, try a series of cover-ups
about your relationship, and include some
misleading information.

Despite the fact that the quiz seems, in its obviousness, like a
joke, Bill Agee would have flunked. His conduct indicated that he
would have answered yes to all the statements.

How two people conduct their private lives is up to them.
However, when a business, its employees, and its stockholders
are affected by what they do, it becomes a public concern. Agee
and Cunningham's naive publicizing of their relationship did a
lot of obvious harm to their corporation and the mentoring system. Because of them, business students and would-be mentors
and protégés already in business and pondering such an arrangement, in many cases are more hesitant to get involved. This
reluctance hurts everyone—the corporation, the potential mentors, and the young executives who need them. It also specifically hurts women, who will find it harder to attract male mentors.

There is little excuse for being unbusinesslike, whether the
protégé is male or female. But sadly, in this case, because the
protégé was a female, the injury runs deep. Professor Clawson, for
one, is hopeful that managers around the country will not draw

the conclusion that it would be too risky to begin a male-female developmental relationship.

Cunningham and Agee "did a great deal of damage," he said. "They probably set that stream of women's influence in managerial positions back five or ten years, in the sense of how male senior managers will feel about having women in managerial positions. Those who think she did well will say, 'Even when you have a competent person, look what trouble you get.' Those who thought she did poorly will say, 'See, I told you so.' In either event, you have a retardation of the process of getting more and more women involved in managerial positions."

"This is one of the awful things about what happened," one person I spoke to lamented. "Many men take Mary Cunningham as a symbol of businesswomen, and this is inaccurate. Mary Cunningham is a person. She is one person among millions of people, and it's unfortunate to let her become a symbol of anything other than that of someone who had no guidelines for conducting her life. She doesn't represent anybody but Mary Cunningham. A dreadful situation with absolutely no guidelines as to what to do."

In the final analysis, it really does not matter whether Agee and Cunningham were sleeping together or not. They chose to act as though they were. When it impinged on the way business was conducted, it became a serious problem that Agee could not see and that Cunningham refused to acknowledge because it would have meant her resignation. But for corporations and their executives to give up on, or pull away from, cross-gender mentor relationships because of an episode like this would be shortsighted, somewhat like banning all automobiles because of one bad accident. All that is needed is experience, thoughtfulness, and the realization that we can be in control of what we do, even when it comes to sex.

Nevertheless, there will continue to be people of both sexes and all ages in business, and many men and women who are not accustomed to it will have to work together. There will be an increasing number of gender-related problems, especially for high-level men who have never dealt with middle- and upper-level women. Romantic ties between senior executives are certain to develop, and rumors of romantic alliances are even more likely, after the Agee notoriety, to wrongly implant themselves in suspicious minds.

# Part 2

THE
SOLUTION

## Chapter 6

# HOW NOT TO RUIN YOUR CAREER—
ADVICE FOR EXECUTIVES

*M* en and women can ruin their careers in a multitude of ways. Poor performance is the most obvious; sexual mismanagement is merely the newest. Our social experience tells us to do one thing, yet our business experience forbids it. How can one manage such disharmony?

What seems to be true one day may well change by the next. Michael E. Meyer, a partner at Lillick McHose and Charles, a prominent Los Angeles law firm, recommended an antidating rule at his company. *The Wall Street Journal* reported him as saying that since "there are 200 million people in the United States, lawyers here surely could go out with someone outside our firm."

Some time after his suggestion had become a company policy, Meyer needed a date for a dinner with a client, asked a female associate lawyer to accompany him, and then fell in love with her. He asked management to reverse the rule—which it did rather than lose either employee. "The policy was so logical and rational, but you forget to be analytical when your heart takes control," said Meyer. He and his new wife both still work at the firm.

## HANDLING YOUR AFFAIR—HOW TO AND
HOW NOT TO

**Case 1:** Joan, who was in middle management, and Pete, in upper management, worked for the same corporation but in different sections. They were in love with each other. Both were excellent workers. One day at lunchtime they ended up alone in a corporate screening room. Thinking everyone was out, they proceeded to make love. It was at that point that someone walked into the screening room by chance.

Fortunately for Joan and Pete, the person did not go rushing off to tell their mutual supervisor. He had enough sensitivity to warn them about their stupidity and lack of professionalism, adding that ten people could have walked into the room instead of one. He asked them never to behave that way again, and pointed out that if they did, he would complain to top management. For the first time, the couple was made to realize they were not exerting any personal control over their behavior, and though others knew about their affair, they were now on the brink of causing tension and discrediting themselves irreparably.

**Case 2:** Larry, one of the officers of a manufacturing corporation, became involved with Kathy, a lower-ranking employee. Due to his help, she suddenly got a terrific promotion in his department. Others in the department became upset and wrote to the president of the parent company. He in turn referred the matter back to the president of the subsidiary company and said, "Handle it in any way you wish." The president decided to let the affair take its own path because Larry was an extremely effective officer. But the letters were talked about and caused embarrassment.

Larry and Kathy became social outcasts. They didn't go to company parties because they were aware of people's attitudes and of the talk behind their backs: "She's getting ahead by sleeping with her boss." The sad part was that Kathy was extremely capable and would have gotten ahead anyway. Larry certainly should not have arranged a promotion for his lover. Sensing the office's disapproval, he should have suggested that she transfer to another department or even find another job if that became necessary.

**Case 3:** A badly managed affair not only distorts the power structure, as in the following case, but it can create an unhealthy atmosphere which leads to further gossip, erroneous accusations, and suspicion. In this example, the affair took place between Steve, a married department head, and Julia, his number-one deputy. Everybody knew about it but pretended they didn't.

She was said to be far brighter than he, and he became dependent on her. Although Steve worshiped Julia, she didn't care nearly as much about him. An executive who worked in the corporation at the time said, "It was a nasty business. There were all sorts of things wrong. He was getting twice his deputy's salary while she was doing the work. People were uncomfortable also because they knew the two of them shared every piece of information and every political strategy. You knew that when you were talking to her, you were also talking to him, and vice versa."

The corporation had a weak president, and was inundated with political maneuvering and sabotage. There were many cliques and factions. The department head protected his deputy and she protected him, and because there were a lot of resources available to them, they presented a formidable obstacle to others in search of authority. They were stronger together than they would have been separately, and in this sense they overwhelmed the normal avenues of power.

The affair made the employees suspicious of one another. For example, a rumor began during this time about two women executives who were close friends. People began to whisper that they were probably lovers. This was not true, but the sport of the moment was to look for liaisons and to make them up if necessary.

Finally the president was forced out by the Board of Directors, and eventually the whole top group left, including Steve and Julia, who went off and started a business of their own.

Theoretically, if the head of a department and the chief deputy are working together, the closer their daily business relationship is the more effective they can be. However, that was not the case here because this couple had something to conceal. And when that something was discovered, it hurt their effectiveness.

Steve and Julia broke one of the cardinal rules. The fact that she reported to him, was evaluated by him, and got her raises from him led to disgruntlement among their colleagues. People perceived him as biased. One or both should have transferred to another part of the corporation or it should have been arranged for Julia to report to someone else.

**Case 4:** Jeff, a high-ranking officer, and Nancy, a manager, were attracted to each other. They did not have an affair because both were married, but the attraction persisted. Then Nancy was moved into a new job which meant she would be working more closely with Jeff. Suddenly his attitude changed. The attraction upset him. He refused to include her in project meetings, he cut short working sessions with her or postponed them, and was stern and snappish with her.

In this case, the mere presence of sexual tension could have hurt Jeff's career because he was not functioning properly. He was unaccustomed to positive feelings toward a working partner, and badly needed some awareness training on how to manage himself when faced with the presence of women, which he should have sought from the company psychologist or counselor.

**Case 5:** Margaret, a personnel director, was in love with Sam, a married man in her corporation who was getting a divorce. When there were business meetings about compensation and Sam's name was likely to be mentioned, she had to bow out because people knew they were having an affair and she could not be seen influencing salary decisions for him. She was not able to do her job properly. Cincinnati-based consultant Kaleel Jamison, who had been hired by this corporation to counsel employees, advised this couple on how to manage themselves in a way that would cause the least possible disruption.

Said Jamison, "I told them, don't call each other at the office, don't go into each other's building, be as discreet as you can be, and realize that as soon as the affair becomes common knowledge a lot of anger is going to be directed at Margaret because of sexism and the fact that Sam is married.

"The other thing I cautioned them about was that just because they were not hearing how people in the organization were reacting did not mean that they were not reacting negatively. It also did not mean that Sam's credibility was not being hurt. Sam is a fairly high-level manager, and men and women were feeling upset and distressed at him for what he was doing."

So Jamison began pushing Margaret to move out of Personnel as quickly as possible, and to a part of the company far away from Sam. If the corporation could not move her laterally, Margaret had to decide that she would be the one to leave because since she was the younger, she could get a job more easily, and Sam's financial compensation package was much more complex than hers.

Aside from being well behaved and sensitive to others' feelings while trying to arrange a transfer or looking for a job elsewhere, there are other ways to handle a corporate romance. You can go around the problem, you can give it up, or you can challenge the restrictions.

**Case 6:** Bill and Phyllis fell in love while working for a manufacturing corporation. They were in the same division but did not report to each other. She was the first woman at the management level in that division, so there were no precedents for helping their supervisor understand their sexual attraction. When they announced they were going to get married, the company's president said, "You can't do that. We can't allow that. One of you will have to leave."

And they said, "Well, we don't want to leave."

"Sorry, those are the rules," the president insisted. He was concerned because they worked with some of the same people. Phyllis felt, however, that for her to have gotten such a high-level job in that corporation was a significant accomplishment, and it wasn't easy to find another job. Bill didn't want to move.

"Okay," they decided, "we won't marry, we'll just live together."

"It blew the boss's mind," Bill said, "because it was a form of rebellion." He couldn't fire them for having a relationship because everybody thought it was wonderful. This resolution to an affair in this corporation worked quite well, and it was finally accepted by everyone.

**Case 7:** In another instance, Sally, a professional in a very large corporation, had a year-long affair with Charlie, her boss and the president of the company. He was married; she was not. Because of the possibility that other people would find out and because of their common concern and their maturity, they concluded that it wasn't worth it.

They ended the affair, but continued to work together for two years afterwards. Their temporary closeness led to an even better working relationship. They were both dedicated to their jobs, spent a lot of time talking about work-related problems, and were able to pour their unexpended sexual energies into their office tasks. It gave them a certain sense of pride to be able to do this as smoothly as they did.

**Case 8:** Often, however, neither lover is married and they would never consider giving up their relationship. They would rather fight for it. When Michael Nelson, the top features editor of *The Kansas City Star*, and Christine Cater, an editor of its Sunday Magazine, fell in love, they were aware of their newspaper's rule which forced one member of the couple to leave if they married after meeting on the job.

According to a report in *The Wall Street Journal*, the couple became engaged and informed their boss that they would not leave their jobs voluntarily. The paper would have to change its policy, or fire them. As a result, the ban on employing spouses was rescinded. But this didn't solve the problem for the lovers because Cater reported to Nelson, and that was still forbidden. The solution came and, in a sense, the victory, when the *Star* removed the magazine, including Cater, from Nelson's supervision, but continued to employ them both in the same jobs.

For the moment, women will have to be particularly careful in certain environments because, as one executive put it, "even if men and women are equal, the guy is more equal than she is." Young executives will have to be aware, too, that although they believe the principle that what they do with their personal lives is their own business, they may erroneously assume that they can do whatever they want, and that it is not going to affect their careers. However, inappropriately handling a romantic attraction may well put a big dent in a career that is just getting started.

This does not mean they should give up an affair or an attraction. It means they must judge their surroundings, perhaps get some advice from a consultant or a trusted colleague, and make a reasonable plan as to how to handle the situation.

## WHEN IT WORKS AND WHEN IT DOESN'T

In trying to best handle an emerging office romance, one must remember that although it is difficult to predict what will happen in certain situations and in certain corporations, some circumstances are universal. According to Karen Brethower, a psychologist and former human resources director at Chase Manhattan, a romance usually does not work when one person reports to the other. That is the most difficult situation and the sort that can create jealousies within the company. Other problem relationships are those where two people work on competitive projects or work for business units that are competing for corporate resources.

It also doesn't work if the couple's behavior is immature and if they bring the relationship into the workplace in an inappropriate way. Says Brethower, "If someone can come in and see that two people are involved in a relationship, it's likely they are engaging in inappropriate behavior."

From the point of view of the corporation, romance will work when careers are not jeopardized. It will work for the couple when there is no opportunity for their professional positions to be compromised by information that either one of them may have and share with the other. Thus, it works most easily when you have two people in low-level positions who aren't privy to a lot of confidential information; it works when you have people in parallel functions with no connection between jobs; it works when they are widely separated—one might be in merchandising, for example, and the other in systems engineering—and not involved with the same products or with the same managers. Above all, the relationship has a better chance of working if the couple maintains a professionalism that cannot be questioned.

## DIFFERENT KINDS OF ATTRACTION

It is crucial to comprehend the fact that there are many kinds of attraction, and that just because one senses a certain amount of magnetism does not mean that one must act on it as though it were love. Being able to distinguish various kinds of feelings, in fact, being able to see that all attraction is not love or even the basis for an affair, will save many a career from self-destructing.

One of the things about all friendships, believes management consultant Nancy Brown, is that sexual attraction is part of it, to some degree or another. "People tend to think of it in terms of either 'I feel' or 'I don't,' whereas I think the reality is that most of us are attracted to many people, and it could be minor or major. But we tend to think the only time it is sexual is when sirens are going off and lights are flashing. So when people, have any strong feelings, they assume it's got to be sexual attraction when quite often it's a lot of other things."

What are these other things? One of the emotions most executives experience is a caring, supportive, *simpatico* feeling toward another colleague that will never include sex, but could be called a type of love. Some executives, on the other hand, seek love for different reasons. Psychiatrist Terence McGuire finds that some people at work get involved sexually because they are fighting off a crushing depression of some kind and this is their way of trying to deal with it. Some people can be involved sexually with someone they actually feel very casual about. "There is so much stuff that is funneled through 'love' that has nothing to do with love, that it is a very complicated area," he says.

The Menninger Foundation's Dr. Meredith Titus also finds that a sexual relationship might be used to respond to needs that are not what we think of when we think of two people having a romance. She says some people will have a sense of loneliness or alienation or tension over power distribution in the group, and will react by developing a sexual relationship to handle it.

She gives the example of a man and a woman who are sharing a job at similar levels of power. They have equal titles, and one of the issues is who is going to be more dominant in the work setting. There is a tension between them just as there might be between two men. But while two men might deal with it by having, say, a vigorous racquetball competition, says Dr. Titus, a man and a woman may develop a sexual relationship and thereby attempt to neutralize their competitiveness.

"In this way," Dr. Titus explained, "love and sexuality are used as tools to deal with other issues."

Dr. Titus sees another such drive for sex when two people are actively involved in challenging work with mutual tasks, learning together, acquiring new skills—all of which leads people to think they have more in common or more of a bond with each other than they actually have, and certainly more than they would have if they were to meet under different circumstances. She said it is analogous to two roommates who live together in a college dorm. Had they met under other circumstances they probably would not have become friends, but as a result of sharing an intense experience, they are drawn to each other. Yet in later years when they get together, they find they really have nothing in common.

For whatever reason one senses a chemistry, the question remains: what do you do about these different kinds of love? Many executives said they would bring it out into the open and talk to the other person about it. Sometimes it may hurt to talk because the other person may not feel the same way, but at least each knows where the other stands.

Consultant Nancy Brown also believes sexual attractions should not be set aside. "I think that pretending that you don't feel attracted to anyone and no one feels attracted to you is pretending something that isn't so. Those feelings will leak out anyway even though they are not managed consciously. That's when it is most destructive, because they get acted out in funny ways."

She believes that thousands of dollars are lost every day through the mismanagement of sexual attraction. In her view, the person who doesn't acknowledge to a co-worker that there are feelings tends to avoid the co-worker. "For example," she said, "say I'm attracted to Bob, but I feel awkward telling him about it so that I consciously or unconsciously avoid being around him because it raises those uncomfortable feelings for me. What happens is that all kinds of information which would normally be shared in a meeting or in a quiet moment in the office don't get shared because I'm not spending the time with him.

"I don't feel easy picking up the phone and saying, 'Hey, what about project 1270 and where are you on that?' It also impinges on giving critical feedback. If I'm attracted to a colleague and haven't expressed that, it would be more difficult to say, 'Hey, I think you screwed up on that part of the project.' "

Brown thinks it is possible to incorporate feelings of sexual magnetism into a friendship in a way that enhances it and one's work. "If you let that part of you flow in a natural, spontaneous way, you are likely to have more fun and be more creative about the kinds of things you say and do."

Men and women must understand that they will be attracted to a lot of people at work, but attraction doesn't need to mean that you end up in bed together, have an affair or a romance that leads to marriage. You could just be friends, acknowledging that you find each other special. Then it will be possible to enjoy one another, have lunches together, not feel unnecessarily tense, and focus the increase in energy that derives from the sexual excitement so that you are more productive on the job.

## PARALLEL ATTRACTIONS

What we are witnessing, then, in addition to a new sexual climate in the office, is the birth of something I call the Sexual Friendship. It consists of a deep sexual attraction (and perhaps love) for someone you are excited by and admire, but someone with whom you wish to share only your business hours. When drawn to another person, we have always assumed a choice had to be made. And we have often made a wrong or stupid choice under the influence of strong emotions. Actually we are capable of simultaneously harboring different quantities and qualities of sexual attraction or love for different people. And it is perfectly possible that you could love your husband or wife and fall in love in a different way with a man or woman colleague. It does not mean that you have to give up either object of your affections. Nor does it mean you have to have sex with the person at work.

Our social history and the myths we have digested have always made us believe there was one right person for each of us, when in fact there are many. If we are lucky enough to know two right people at the same time, we can express this caring in different ways and in different places without obliterating our marriages or careers, to satisfy our normal physical drives. Rather than thinking in terms of extramarital attraction, which carries an unsavory connotation, I prefer to call it a Parallel Attraction. You live with one of your lovers, have your children or social life with that one, and you can work with, and are simply very close to, your second love, the important friend in your life whom you care about quite separately.

## DECIDING IN ADVANCE

If you want your career to go smoothly and your sexual attractions or romances to work, you must make certain decisions, preferably before you become too deeply involved to be able to handle the situation. For example, one director of human resources suggested that if two people become attracted they should discuss how they are going to deal with it if it falls apart. That is something one can afford to ignore in the usual social context, but not when the attraction is in the office. "They should talk about it up front, and come up with some parameters on themselves," the director said, such as, "If we break up, then you will do this and I will do that." Maybe one will agree to move, or they might decide, "We're not going to be bitter. We will behave in such-and-such a way."

It may sound cold to plan for love-related catastrophes in advance, but if you don't, this executive advised, you're going to be caught up short. If you are in a meeting and your lover challenges one of your ideas, he or she wouldn't want you to take it personally. Things like that can cause problems unless they are talked through, and exactly the same thing will happen in sexual situations.

It is necessary to consider how you wish to respond to your

company culture if it happens to have a more narrow-minded concept of employee behavior than you do. You should decide in advance just where your priorities are. What are the reasons for working? What is important to you? What will you give up if necessary?

Would he say, "I'm not going to give up love for some stupid corporate policy"? Or would she say, "My career is too important to give up for any amount of love"? Or would they decide to go live in the South Seas? As social psychologist and consultant Dr. Jennifer Macleod puts it, "There are more options than people realize. But there are always trade-offs. People have varying commitments to their careers, and various reasons for having them. Why do you want to get ahead—money, status, or power? Perhaps you want to show your brothers or sisters you can do better than they did. Or is it so you can feel good even if you don't have kids?"

If your career came first, and you thought it would damage your career, you'd cut off the love affair. The best thing a person can do, Dr. Macleod says, is to have a clear view of what he or she wants—and believes is possible—and base the decision on that view and not on what the rules ought to be.

One thing to consider, even in the best of all possible companies, is whether or not you have unwittingly put yourself on the fast track to a lot of unforeseen problems. If you are having a romance and it's okay with the corporation, there still may be quicksand up ahead. If you both were promoted, it could be more and more difficult to avoid overlapping responsibilities. Rather than waiting for that to occur, two officers embarking on a romance should discuss such eventualities and decide whether, when, and who would move to avoid it.

Black businessmen and businesswomen must make special decisions to protect their careers. A black female executive told me that many white men have fantasies about sleeping with black women, and vice versa. "If I had an affair with a white man," she said, "I'd be living up to some of the perceptions white people have about black women, that is, that they are promiscuous. It's not that I *think* white men think black women are promiscuous. I *know*. I've had a lot of black-white awareness training, and that sort of thing comes out in those sessions—what blacks and whites think of each other." So she decided at the beginning that "there was no way I was going to fulfill anybody's fantasies or conceptions. I was not ready to put my career on the line. It is hard enough in the corporation being black and a woman." She has been approached by both black and white men. "To even think of doing something like that with a white man would be absolutely crazy," she said. "It would be suicidal."

As psychologist and consultant Karen Brethower puts it, you either allow yourself an in-company relationship or you forbid it and choose to have your relationships outside the workplace. "And that choice, however you make it, is a significant one," she said. "My recommendation is that people make it consciously rather than just let it happen. I know that's a very rational thing to say," she continued, "but I think that is the best approach."

It should be said that any decision based on controlling the emotions is always subject to sudden reversal. We all remain human and therefore vulnerable, but at least thinking about which way to go and devising a plan to give yourself direction if confronted with an emotional situation will make work relationships less threatening and provide a framework for turning love off, if that seems best. It also will help people protect their careers from responses to an unplanned personal dilemma for which they are unprepared.

## PROVING YOU ARE SERIOUS

One of the most crucial elements to help protect a career, but also one of the most intangible, is how you are perceived. If you are turning in a splendid performance, the supervisors will be far more apt to look the other way if your romantic life is not exactly what they think it should be. A magnificent professional job carries a lot of weight, while a marginal one will give them an excuse to get rid of you. If your romantic life bothers them, and your professional production is only fair, they will add the two up and say, Why bother? Such a person isn't worth the investment.

As one executive put it, "You can't let them come back and nitpick at stuff that you are not doing in your job and use that as leverage to get back at you. Then you're in trouble. You've got to keep yourself airtight."

The corporate establishment's inclination when confronted by a sexual situation is to point a finger at the woman. The stereotypes are so habitual that at times even a female supervisor will fall victim to them. In one instance, a young executive was about to marry an officer in a bank where they both worked. She complained, "I had to prove to my female supervisor that I should still be taken seriously even though I was getting married. She warned me that someone else had gotten married and hadn't done her job properly for three months before or after, and I should realize the department was extremely sensitive to this." The young woman became so upset by her supervisor's admonitions that she began working until eight every evening.

"It's the assumption about any woman with a career," she said, "that you won't work if you marry and that as soon as you marry you will probably have children and quit. So you have to work twice as hard to prove that romance and marriage aren't obliterating your career desires."

## SEXUAL OFFICE BEHAVIOR—A CHECKLIST

The following assorted reminders on how to deal with a relationship in the office might save your career. Many of them have been discussed earlier. Though some may not seem any of the company's business, during this transition period, one will either have to adhere to them, or take the risks that pioneering new concepts has always entailed.

- Decide in advance whether you will have a relationship if the opportunity arises. If you wait until you are involved, it will be too thorny to extricate yourself easily.
- People *are* capable of rational decisions about relationships. You have the power at the beginning to turn them off.
- Don't be afraid to simplify your life by refusing to get involved in a sexual liaison you might like. With a little discipline you can refuse. Draw the line. If it's not worth it, say so.
- If someone hassles you with comments such as, "Let's get it on together," or, "You're turning me on," say, "Hey, wait a minute. I don't do that," or "Hey, I can appreciate that. It's a nice compliment, but I'm not interested." Have the guts to say what you think.
- If you wish to discourage a romantic relationship in the office, start talking about a husband, or a boyfriend or girlfriend, even if that person doesn't exist. If the person does exist, talk about something you did together. This will reinforce the signals. Especially if you are a woman, whether the relationship gets started and how far it goes is still your problem and responsibility. Develop a technique that you find works.
- Never, ever, have a relationship with a person you report directly to. If you really want it, move elsewhere.
- Do not have a relationship in a company unless you can stay far enough away from each other so your work won't be influenced by the other person.
- Don't get involved with anyone in Personnel, unless one of you is willing to move. Some companies will demand this.

- Do not have a romance with a married colleague unless you are prepared for a lot of messy office gossip. The judgment will be that you are stealing your friend away from his or her spouse. Even in these days of liberated relationships, people still tend to be protective about the institution of marriage. If the marriage is bad, get the divorce and then have your affair. As some wise person once said, "Either fish or cut bait." Corporations are conservative on this issue, and your wisdom will be questioned: "If he [she] would do that, what else would he [she] do?"
- If your affair creates an obvious conflict of interest, and the love is more important to you than the company, don't be afraid to act quickly and look for another job.
- In a difficult romantic situation, don't wait until the corporation asks you to leave or move. By that time, more damage will have been done to you than you will be able to rectify easily. Take the initiative and avoid all the unpleasantness that usually takes place when the company finally steps in.
- If you have a painful breakup with someone at the office, don't allow yourself to obsess about something that didn't work. Find some other activity that's meaningful and time-consuming. Take on new challenges. It's not easy, but redirecting your thoughts will help, especially if you have been dumped. Another solution is to pour your energies into your work in a way that is constructive and will get you positive feedback. This is difficult because your energy is lower when you are depressed. However, it will help if you work on other relationships and friendships where people really like you, inside or outside the office. Try to realize that if the other person didn't think the affair was that great, he

171

or she would not be able to give you what you want in the long run.

- If your affair breaks up, try eventually to establish a relationship with the person similar to those you have with colleagues of your own sex. It may be strained and formal at first, but if you keep at it, it will probably become a friendship worth having and will enable you to work together.
- If you are in a corporation that you think tolerates personal male-female relationships, and you begin one but you still feel uneasy, go to your supervisor and say that you wanted him or her to know about the relationship in case anyone should mention it, and that you will be scrupulously careful. Ask to be informed if you are getting into a conflict-of-interest situation. Then go ahead and enjoy the love affair outside of working hours.
- Be sensitive to others' feelings at work. They may be lonely, jealous of your talents, ambitious. If you give them reason to gossip about you, it will lead to a situation you won't be able to control.
- Try to get some clue about your supervisor's personal values so that you don't unintentionally offend him or her.
- Tie yourself into a support network to find out how other men and women have handled romantic situations at your company. Know what the precedents are so you don't make mistakes.
- If you are a woman, realize that men prefer *you* to initiate handshakes so as not to appear to be flirtatious.
- The more flirtatious he or she gets, the more business-like you should get.
- Use your body language as well as your words to turn a man or woman off. Look away, lean back, cross your arms, check your watch.

- If you feel the need to turn someone off, try to do it without hurting his or her ego. If you put your colleague down crudely, you won't be able to work together comfortably.
- If several women attend a meeting with many men, they should split up and sit at different parts of the table so men cannot focus hostility on women as the other sex.
- Be like Caesar's wife—above reproach. It is not enough that you are not having an affair; you must also give the appearance of not being interested.
- If your supervisor is suddenly beginning to find fault with your work and you are having a romance, beware. This is probably a sign that the company doesn't like it and is trying to tell you—or get rid of you.
- If you are in love, don't get light-headed because you feel great. Unfortunately, people often look for such an opportunity to get back at you, and will find your overt happiness offensive.
- If you have a romance, take advantage of the fact that it can be healthy and that you can learn a lot from the other person about the company, your career, and life.
- If your private life is a problem for your supervisor, there are options available to you. You can move to another part of the company, move to another company, or leave and start a company of your own. If you are in a very specialized field or your desires are so focused that you have your heart set on being president of Old Blue Chip Bank and they happen to have a no-fraternization policy, then you'll be disappointed. Otherwise, there are plenty of other banks, law firms, manufacturing companies, or whatever.
- If you are just out for a good time, avoid an affair. They are disrupting, distracting, and bad for morale. If your

intentions are honorable, and you are prepared to pursue the relationship in a serious way, then go ahead.

- Consider keeping your relationship secret until you see how serious it is going to be, so that if it turns out to be only temporary, others will not make judgments.
- Lobby in your state legislature for a Corporate Love Law so people can be protected from being fired for living with a person of the opposite sex or for having a private office romance.
- Make sure the corporation realizes you are spending your time on business, even if you have a romance. E.g., don't communicate through the computer system.
- Understand that there are two elements to career success. One is your actual performance; the other is how you are perceived. A flirtatious person who is not having an affair may incur harsher judgment than a discreet person who is. Be massively professional at all times.
- Bend over backward not to impede your lover's ability to work. He or she wants to be recognized as a professional. Show professional consideration to your lover.
- Beware of nineteenth-century-type managers. Be circumspect and don't advertise your relationship, even if you don't have to keep it secret, because you can never tell who might have a negative reaction even though it appears no one around you will.
- Don't allow yourself to be distracted when your lover is in the office. Don't spend time wandering the halls past offices to get a glimpse of your friend.
- If you are the vulnerable type and think it would be difficult for you to handle an office romance, look outside your business for social friends.
- A large percentage of romantic love is made up of fantasy. Be more analytical about the facts of your attraction.

- Guard against infatuation with power. If you fall in love with a title and fantasize about the person, you may later find out that he or she is not all the person you thought.
- Know your company policy. This seems obvious, but a lot of people don't find out until it's too late. If you are not sure what the written rules are, ask your supervisor for a copy.
- You're not in high school anymore. No necking around the water cooler, closet, stockroom, under the desk, or any other nook and cranny you can find.
- Be aware that as a woman in a male organization, you will have more attention paid to what you do. If you date three men during a year and your male counterpart dates three women, he will be perceived as a man's man, a guy who really gets around. Men will envy him. You will be perceived as loose, and the connection will be made to poor business judgment. This may not be fair, but in many companies it is the reality.
- Don't use an affair to get ahead. It may well backfire and stunt a career that was moving fast without it. Use your brains rather than your sex to negotiate your advancement.
- When men start telling dirty jokes about what this woman or that one would be like in bed, either keep quiet and listen or tell the men you are not in the mood. It is a compliment if they think you are one of the guys and forget a woman is present.
- If you have an affair and others are jealous because "he picked her instead of me," or "she chose him instead of me," that's the other person's problem. Just make sure your behavior is professional and ignore the catty remarks.
- Live with the fact that some people see each other more

and exchange more information because they are lovers, mentor and protégé, married, or buddies. Everybody knows that happens. Don't feel guilty if you are in such a situation.

- If you are having an affair and you both want to work together, look for a collaborative part of the business where sharing information would be seen as a benefit rather than a loss.
- Women, keep your own name. It is usually best not to take on your husband's name if you work for the same company. While it may at times be more confusing if people don't know you are married, having separate names avoids raising the specter of two people constantly exchanging information. It also gives the woman a more independent, professional appearance among her colleagues.
- Corporate couples should realize they are not going to be able to sail through their careers and remain equal at all times. Opportunities will come up for one and not the other. Decide in advance how you wish to handle such a situation, so that you are not in constant competition with each other.
- Don't go to restaurants, movies, or cultural or sports events with a working colleague of the opposite sex unless you don't care if people jump to conclusions or gossip.
- If you do go to a restaurant with a colleague of the opposite sex and wish to avoid gossip, keep a lot of papers on the table so it looks as though you are having a business meeting. Shuffle them occasionally.
- If everyone is going to a meeting at a resort with his or her spouse, and you are a divorcee who will be seen as a threat by the other husbands and wives, take a friend or a son or daughter so people can see you either as

someone who is not looking because you have a companion, or as a responsible parent who is busy with a child in the evenings.

- If you and your lover are going to a dinner or social function associated with business, treat each other with more reserve than you would if your friend were from outside the company.
- Don't have lunch with your lover. Have it with business colleagues.
- If you have a dinner meeting with a colleague of the opposite sex, simply go your way when dinner is over and let the other person do the same. This will give you the freedom to have evening meetings without sexual implications being attached to them.
- If you are a woman executive, get to know the wives of your male colleagues. Invite couples over for dinner so they see that you are not seeking a romantic relationship with their spouses and that you value them as well.
- If you are a woman, think of conventions as regular work time, because it's the woman who will get chastised if there's any playing around. If you feel a situation is getting out of hand and the perceptions of what's going on won't look good for you, withdraw and go back to your room.
- Be careful of Christmas and other office parties. Your behavior is always being observed by someone. Be aware and make choices; don't just do things out of habit or because you feel like it at the moment. There are times when you may go ahead and do something anyway, even though you know there may be a penalty attached to it, because you think it's worth it. But make sure you think of the consequences in advance, before the first drink, and make a conscious choice about what you will or will not do.

- Be consistent. If you are the affectionate kind who likes to slap someone on the shoulder or hug, do it to everyone you like; don't single out one person, because that will just feed the gossip grapevine.

## WHAT TO DO ABOUT GOSSIP

Gossip is one of the most intangible, insidious forces in any office. It breeds on perceptions, whether they are true or not. It uses jealousy as a tool to tarnish reputations. It is embroidered upon as it goes from mouth to mouth, so that often the final commentary has little to do with the original information. It is mischievous. But it is delicious fun, and everybody loves it. Exposing secret information about an employee gives the person who has the inside scoop a certain amount of clout. Having this power makes people feel more important and takes the boredom out of a routine day.

You can stop other people from gossiping by starving them of information about you. If you do nothing suggestive, they have nothing to feed on. In preventing gossip, it is important that in your day-to-day behavior you make your intentions clear. If others see you as a flirtatious person, they will imagine that a lot more is going on. However, remember that a certain amount of gossip is unavoidable no matter how circumspect you are because of the nature of business and the persistence of stereotypes. Many people will automatically assume, for example, that if a man and a woman go off on a business trip together, they must be sleeping together.

One female executive averted gossip by her straightforward behavior. She was in a business where she had to travel with men colleagues to call on her clients around the country.

"There were times when I would drive over to pick the guy up at his house, and there would be his wife and kids, and we'd say goodbye and drive off into the sunset together. The wives knew me and knew I had no interest in their husbands. My job was my job, and I wasn't on the make for every guy just because I went away with him for a couple of days of business." She made that fact clear to the men, their wives, and her other colleagues, and people didn't gossip about her because her intentions were not suspect.

Many a senior executive is afraid to take an attractive junior executive of the other sex to lunch, drinks, dinner, or on a trip, fearing the harm gossip can do.

"It's impossible to keep other people from talking," a banker who married another banker in the same corporation told me. "Just don't worry about it. If you are going to live your whole life worrying about what other people might say about you, that's a little crazy because you can never be one step ahead of the gossip. So I would say, forget about what others are saying, and do whatever you feel is right and feel comfortable with. Try to keep your office romance out of the office and that will keep the gossip down."

Nancy Brown said she had several long-term nondating friendships with male colleagues in a corporation. There was talk. "I didn't do anything to feed those rumors," she said, "but I didn't want to live my life in fear of working with those men because of what somebody was going to think." So she ignored the gossip, though she and her male colleagues would occasionally joke about it: "You want to start a rumor? Let's close the door."

I think this attitude makes sense. Given that gossip damages a career, and that interaction between men and women is essential to good business, the best one can do without living in hermetic isolation is to go about one's work properly, be friendly but businesslike, joke without being suggestive, be one's natural self, and hope that one's colleagues will have more important things to talk about.

179

## TO BE OR NOT TO BE—SECRETIVE

There is a strong difference of opinion among executives and management consultants regarding whether or not a couple having a romantic relationship should reveal it. Curiously, perhaps because they are frightened of violating the unwritten corporate rules or have heard too many horror stories, most of the executives I spoke to seemed to feel that keeping an affair secret was safer. Many were successful in doing so, though consultants say it is close to impossible to hide. Whether their superiors knew or guessed was sometimes open to question, but they were so discreet that no one said anything to them. On the other hand, most of the human resource officers and consultants who have done counseling in this area feel that keeping it a secret is the wrong path to take, and could be dangerous.

Chapter 4 dealt with the story of Sue and Jim, who kept their affair a secret for six years and thus were able to work together. But in the case of Jon Slohoda, who kept his affair secret from United Parcel Service, pandemonium broke loose when they found out. So for him, keeping his personal life a secret was only a temporary solution that postponed the inevitable.

Being secretive and then being discovered can cause many complications. Take the example of a woman technician at a scientific organization who was receiving outstanding performance ratings. The company rarely gave so high an evaluation, and she had been getting them for some time. At one point her supervisor was asked by management to move to another part of the company. It's a large corporation, but he didn't want to move and they couldn't figure out why. It wasn't a promotion, but it positioned him for one later.

Then they found out what the other technicians already knew, that this man and woman had been living together for over a year, although they drove to work in different cars and left work at different times. Once the story was out, the woman's performance dropped significantly. Management was furious. They didn't know whether or not the man had falsified her performance ratings. They were angry with him for not being straightforward, and with her because they couldn't accurately judge whether or not she really was exceptional. They therefore couldn't plan for her future with the company. And the other technicians complained. "We were treated unfairly," they said. "She's been having this affair with him all along. What has this meant in terms of our assignments and performance ratings?"

Wharton's Professor Jerome Katz points out that in such a situation, you are violating the norms of the organization by having the relationship. Then if you keep it to yourself, you are actually breaking two rules: you are living together, and you are lying to the organization. You break a rule, then you camouflage the violation. "Then you have to camouflage the fact that you are camouflaging. It builds, and the longer you do this without telling, the more it will exacerbate the problem when it comes out."

One young couple were peers and had just started dating when he was promoted to manager of their team. When it happened, the woman spoke to consultant Kaleel Jamison and told her that she didn't know what to do. The relationship had not developed enough so that they knew whether it would become permanent. The organization had some clear policies against such superior-subordinate situations. She told Jamison that they didn't want to break up the relationship because it might lead to something good for them. She asked what they should do.

Jamison told her it was easier to find another place in the organization, or another job, than it is to find someone you want to spend your life with. She then suggested that since her friend, the manager, had a higher rank, he should go to his superior and be frank about what was happening, talk about the relationship's being new, and say that it might lead nowhere or it might develop into something, but that it was too soon to tell. He should continue by telling his superior that if a performance appraisal had to be done on his friend during this period, he would not do it. Or he would be very careful about how he did it, being sure to get input from others.

Then, said Jamison, the manager should suggest a time frame of perhaps three months after which everyone would look at the situation again. If the relationship looked as if it might blossom, then the woman or the manager would move to some other part of the system so they were not in the same functional line. If the relationship ended, no issue would have been created.

Most of the executives gave the opposite advice. One said, "Keep your relationships secret. How people respond to you is different if they know you have a link to someone else in the corporation, regardless of how remote."

Another remarked, "If you are having an affair, there is nothing to be won for anybody by making it public. It just diverts time and energy—it's that simple."

"Try to keep it a secret," agreed this executive. "Even if you are single, it is still awkward. The more discreet you are, the better off you are. And if you are married, it's really important."

Others agreed:

"Handle the affair as discreetly as possible and tell as few people as possible. Keep it secret. Never go to a supervisor."

"I would assess very quickly whether this is a short- or long-term proposition. If it is going to be short term, don't tell anybody. Everybody fools around, but you don't want anyone to know about it. If it is long term, come out of the closet and tell people."

"No, don't go to a supervisor. If there is no conflict of interest, it's nobody's business but your own."

And finally, "If two people fall in love, I suggest one transfer or leave. It's not always easy, because in some fields, jobs are not that easy to come by. But failing that, if you don't leave, you keep it a secret. I mean, learn how to do it, for God's sake. Don't get caught."

Who's right? The consultants say you should be able to go to your supervisor and get help in handling your affair in the best possible way. If you don't and they find out, you're in real trouble. The executives say okay, but most of them know as little about handling such situations as you do. So keep it to yourself.

If the corporate culture allowed it, it would be best to be able to tell anyone about your relationship and enjoy it in public in a natural way. But that is forbidden in some companies. And even in companies that don't make a fuss over your private life, you might just have a supervisor who is sticky on such subjects, whose morals or ethics will get in the way so that he or she may make life difficult for you.

Thus the only possible advice is to find out just what your company's unwritten rules about fraternization are, and whether you have a manager who will understand if you need to talk. Then decide where your priorities are in case you find yourself in such a situation. Know whether you want career or love to come first at this moment in your life, then devise your own formula. But in general, the more honest you can be about all facets of your life, the better for you and your company. If you can't be honest, you either live with it or think about changing companies.

## TRAVEL TIPS

Business travel leads to easily mismanaged career situations, and male and female colleagues traveling together must monitor their behavior. You both are doing business, you are moving your career ahead, and you are breaking down the stereotypes. Here are some tips to help you:

- If a visit to a client can be managed within one day, don't stay overnight.
- If company travel is necessary, make sure it justifies you and your business-lover traveling jointly. Otherwise it will seem as though you are just looking for a way to

spend some time together. The organization will probably pick up on such "necessary" travel sooner or later.
- If you want to be supercareful in a hostile corporate
environment, don't sit near each other on the plane.
- Arrange it so you do not have connecting or adjoining
hotel rooms and that you don't arrive in and leave the
lobby at the same moment.
- Never share a room, even if you are lovers. Take two
rooms—on different floors, if possible—and sleep in
one.
- Avoid meetings in closed hotel bedrooms unless there
are others present. If that is not possible, arrange to
meet in the hotel's public areas, such as the lobby or
coffee shop.
- Do not assume that because you are out of town, you
are invisible. Sooner or later you will run into your boss,
your boss's secretary, your friend's ex-wife, or someone
else who will be delighted to send the story back home.
(You are not even safe in a foreign city. I know two
corporate lovers who, to their total consternation,
bumped into someone from their own company on a
street in Paris.)
- If you are a female, don't stay up late at night drinking
with a male colleague. Retire early unless there are
others present.
- Don't go to a place for dinner that has music and
dancing. If you do, you are setting up a situation that
is very much like a date and hard to manage. But if you
are in that position and someone says, "Let's dance,"
say, "No thank you" unless you are old friends and your
colleagues perceive you as such, and you know that
nothing will happen. Even so, it still could be risky. If
there is not enough rumor to feed on that week, some
gossipers may simply use your innocent relationship on

the dance floor as proof of a wrongdoing they had suspected all along.

- Don't assume that your relationship will remain undiscovered. According to *Business Week,* Richard E. Tunison, personnel manager of the Atlantic Richfield Company in Los Angeles, was dating another ARCO employee. The two were scheduled to attend a Dallas seminar. They took separate planes and stayed in separate hotels. For their only meal together, they chose a quiet, out-of-the-way restaurant, only to find eight ARCO employees seated at the next table
- Carry your own bags.
- Pay your own restaurant, hotel, and cab bills.
- If you are a male about to go off on a business trip with a female colleague, gracefully announce to your wife that it's just business. Then check in with her by phone often enough to reassure her.

## THE DYNAMICS OF DRESSING

Executives are expected to dress well, and different industries have their own dress codes. The relaxed dress code that may exist in an advertising company won't apply on Wall Street. The company culture will tell you what is expected, and a cursory look around the office will make it even clearer. You don't want to be seen as someone who lacks the taste and judgment to advance in the company.

Women certainly don't have to neutralize or deny their sexuality, or wear a "dress-for-success" suit. Any kind of situation where people feel they have to disguise themselves in order to be acceptable is intrinsically not a good situation to be in. This does not mean that a woman should wear a red chiffon dress with a plunging neckline to her job at Merrill Lynch, any more than a man should wear his madras slacks to his job at Westinghouse. You have to be who you are, but you have to modify it to fit your surroundings, just as you would in any social situation. Within the constraints there is room to show your own personality.

Here are some comments by executives who have had experience dressing with the proper, not-too-sexy wardrobes.

- Try to look attractive but not sexy.
- Make sure you fit into your office environment. Notice what people one level above you wear.
- When you look in the mirror you should like what you see. It should not be in conflict with who you are.
- Your clothes should not distract observers from your job. If you are going to make a speech, you want people to listen to your words. If you are confident about who you are, then you should wear something attractive but fairly inconspicuous. What you want to come out is you, not the purple spots on your skirt or the reflection of your jewelry in the otherwise subdued light of the meeting room.

An advertising executive said, "I don't see any problem with looking as feminine as I can if it will help get the deal or the sale, as long as I'm not hopping in and out of bed with people. But if I know I look best in a red dress, I don't see any problem with wearing it for a specific meeting to get a sale. For me, that's not compromising myself. I'm going to do whatever I can do to turn in the results."

In short, observe others in the company where you work, or ask a colleague, so you can know what codes exist. Conforming while still in the lower management ranks makes sense. Later on, when you are closer to the top and the company can't do without you, more color and frivolity may be acceptable. A suit is not the only possibility for a woman. Conservative dresses and quiet earth colors are probably most conducive to offices that are not primarily artistic and creative. The main point is not to look sexy or provocative; you won't be admired for it. Your individuality should be expressed through your work, not your clothes.

Clothes are just one part of the impression we make on others. Consultant Arleen LaBella believes that 65 percent of what we communicate to people is nonverbal, but the entire message is sent by more than how we dress or stand. It is through patterns of behavior that we communicate.

"Many women tell me they are afraid to make eye contact with a man because they are afraid he'll get the wrong impression. But it's not the eye contact that is going to do that. It's the combination of the eye contact, the lilting voice, the swaying on one hip, the cocked head, the smile. All these things give the message and communicate whether you are interested in sex or not."

What can executive men and women do when people misinterpret how they are dressing or acting? For example, if a woman gives her hand to a man to shake and he not only takes her hand but leans over and kisses her or puts his arm around her, what should her response be?

According to Arleen LaBella, you become more businesslike. You don't say, "I don't want you to do that." And you don't change the subject by becoming personal and saying, "How was your vacation?"

Rather, you should react with a business comment such as, "The project I was hoping we could work on today is . . ." so that everything about you is a subtle message of what you want that relationship to be. "You ignore what he did," advises LaBella, "and you don't comment because it will only increase the intensity between you."

She believes that men and women should not hesitate to shake hands in the office, and that a simple handshake often fosters a work relationship. It says, "I acknowledge you and me as equal contributors in the workplace," and it defines what the relationship is going to be. "I've had men tell me," she said, "that they find it extremely relieving to have a woman do that because it tells them exactly where they stand with her."

What do you do when a man or woman in your office becomes too flirtatious? LaBella suggests that you say, "That's very flattering, but I make it my policy never to mix my business relationships with my personal relationships." But you say it in a kind way. "The worst thing we can do is to get hostile about such things. To be totally honest and totally kind at the same time is crucial."

Furthermore, always be aware of the complete package you wish to present. It is far too easy for others to misinterpret what you are unless you yourself know and control exactly what sort of impression you're out to make.

# Chapter 7

# HOW TO DEAL WITH ROMANCE—
## ADVICE FOR CORPORATIONS

$\mathscr{A}$s employees struggle with the urgent need to create more imaginative male-female relationships, corporations must also make compelling changes that recognize the new realities.

In general, male-female problems among one's employees are a nonsubject. Business concerns seem uppermost in the minds of supervisors, vice presidents, and presidents. But every corporation knows other days when the human entanglements get out of hand, directly affect production, and have to be dealt with rapidly. As we have seen, corporate romance, if not managed, can create major problems.

Just as executives often find themselves awkward in handling their own male-female relationships in the office, so the corporation doesn't have any better notion of how to deal with those who get involved. The corporation has never sat down and studied the matter because it is one of those embarrassing subjects that it can't really get hold of. It's in the realm of human strategy, and can't be added up on a calculator. No corporate officer has ever taken a course in it, ever seriously thought about it, or ever learned anything concerning it. How does one calculate the vagaries of human nature? How does one estimate the shifting realities of human emotion?

When a romance becomes known through observation, gossip, or confession, managers are immediately placed in the position of having to make a decision. Do they do something about it or ignore it? The script hasn't been written. Everyone is ad-libbing. The couple may be secretive, the supervisors anxious and perplexed about what to say to them, and worried about their own jobs if their subordinates don't perform. They must consider what company policy is, what their personal ethics dictate, and hold this up against the fact that now, in the mid-1980s, most people believe their personal lives are their own business. It's a threatening issue.

In discussing office romance, every consultant and every executive with whom I spoke agreed that supervisors do not know how to cope with the problem. Massachusetts management consultant Rick Driscoll said, "It is difficult for our whole society to talk about sexual issues. And male managers, in particular, are not adept at talking about highly personal subjects. But I don't think such matters are any different or any worse than many of the other things we deal with. It's just that we are not used to mixed sexes in the organization. We've just got to develop our skills at this."

"I turn a blind eye," the head of a New England manufacturing company told *Business Week* magazine. "I wouldn't know what to do if I saw something."

A male vice president also admitted that most supervisors can't cope with such situations. "We try to train them to administer the day-to-day problems. But if they have their wits about them and are reasonably human, they should be able to bumble through and then go to company professionals, medical staff, or counselors for expert help."

A senior male manager said, "I don't know of any supervisor who has ever had any training in how to handle this. Occasionally companies have established corporate guidelines on the issue, so people will take out their guidebook and try to figure out what they ought to be doing," he continued. "I guess we all bring our own morality to the situation. If you ask a hundred people, you are going to get a hundred suggestions for solving the problem. An affair is just one kind of disruption in a department."

A Midwestern executive thought supervisors should do more

counseling. "I know we don't. It's not only this corporation, it's a lot of corporations. It's very difficult to sit down with people and talk about personal problems. Most people are very uncomfortable with that. They say, 'I'm not a psychologist.' But if you are going to take on the responsibility of supervising people, then you've got to take on the people's problems with it and learn how to handle them." This executive thought supervisors should receive counseling, too. "That's part of the problem with women in business. Men just don't know how to handle them this way. They can tell their wives to sit down and shut up, but they can't do that with a female employee."

Rick Driscoll remarked that a great deal has to do with the manager's creativity, emotional stability, and the ability to listen, to empathize, and to give constructive suggestions. Most can't do this.

Fellow consultant Jeanne Driscoll pointed out that "managers are appointed because they are skillful technicians in some way. They have been successful and they have track records. Some are very puritanical, old school, religious, and believe in a strict separation between business and pleasure. There are a lot of sexists, too. There may be fewer among the young, but there are a lot who are still going to the strip joints on business trips."

It seems to me that corporations could well afford the cost of training their managers in human sensitivity and behavior skills so they can be effective when they are needed. Not to do this leaves them unnecessarily vulnerable.

## STRATEGIES FOR SUPERVISORS

Unfortunately, many corporations don't consider family problems an appropriate domain for a manager even if, say, an employee's child is on drugs and it's affecting the employee's work. Until the employee's work is massively affected, the manager is supposed to pretend the problem isn't there.

The "we're invincible" image is fine until the weakness in the system shows up, and then anything can happen. As corporate consultant Kaleel Jamison astutely suggests, the only hope a supervisor or a company has of managing a situation so that it does not become a public embarrassment or a productivity drain is to understand the proper techniques for dealing with incidents of sexual attraction when they occur.

Jamison says that a manager's handling of such attraction should be determined by several factors, such as whether there has been any overt behavior, whether a relationship has actually begun, whether the pair is violating some organizational taboo, whether they are being discreet, and how much gossip and distraction exist in the rest of the organization because of the couple's actions.

**Simple Attraction.** Take the common case of sexual attraction that has not yet been acted on, and results in an uneasy working relationship between two people. Jamison advises that the manager casually but gently mention to each person separately what has been observed. If the two deny there is a problem, the manager should say, "Don't discount the possibility of sexual attraction. When two attractive, competent people work together, it often happens, and isn't immediately recognizable. Sometimes it shows up as conflict in the relationship, or an inability to be articulate, or a self-consciousness you never had before."

According to Jamison, the manager should encourage both parties to consider attraction as the root of the problem, to see it as a compliment to the other person, and to discuss the matter with one another in order to dispel the tension. If they can't talk about it together, at least being able to talk confidentially with their supervisor should help.

If the sexual attraction does not take the form of the two snapping at each other, and is recognized by both as a positive affection, the supervisor may still decide to discuss it with each person, because if the supervisor has observed it then others will too, and the couple should be counseled on how to mesh this personal development with their business lives to cause the fewest problems, or none at all.

**The Active Affair.** If the relationship has begun, the manager's role should be human and supportive. Jamison again advises that the two people be approached separately. Because of the awkwardness of such a personal discussion, it simply is easier to talk to people individually. The major responsibility, Jamison believes, should rest with the higher-ranking person, and that person should be approached first.

"Tell the person there is a need to talk about a situation that could be disrupting to the organization," she advises. Make clear that there is no intention of imposing any value judgments on what has happened. The manager should then, says Jamison, analyze and describe clearly:

- The effect on the organization. Are projects behind schedule? Are mistakes being made? Is a lot of organizational energy going into gossip? Describe the problems being caused.
- The effect the affair is having on careers. What is the next step in this person's career, and will the affair impede it? Will decisions on salaries, promotions, assignments, and career mobility be influenced by the affair? Does the romance involve someone in a direct management line? Suggest a transfer or a different assignment for a year. Talk about what can be done and the career implications.

After the manager talks one-on-one to each person, advises Jamison, then the three should meet together. Although the supervisor's job is to protect the interests of the organization and make sure there is no disruption, the task should be approached in a helpful and supporting way. The lovers and their supervisor should discuss the options, and the supervisor should urge both people to sort out their own values and make their own choices after considering the consequences of any action or nonaction they might agree on.

Jamison observes that the couple's response to such a discussion may be unpredictable, but most people will be confused, have doubts about what they are doing, and will be grateful and relieved to talk about it. Defusing sexual attraction early, she says, will cause the least damage.

Jamison also points out that when the attraction begins, there is a period when one or both parties may be less productive because they are expending energy wondering, "How are we going to get together?" "Does he like me?" "Does she like me?" Therefore she would advise the manager to give the couple a chance to get over their initial excitement, because in the long run their happiness could result in increased productivity.

An executive with a lot of experience in this area gave his advice on what should take place. The ideal situation, he thought, would be for the supervisor to say, "Look, I think something is affecting, if not your actual performance, than at least its perceived contribution. In the interest of your career and my career, since I'm responsible for the work of this unit, I'd really like you to find an alternative to what's going on."

Instead, what usually happens, according to this executive, is that the supervisor, who will have ignored the problem for as long as possible, will activate his or her on-off switch, and take some action like sitting them down and saying, "Stop it!" Or even more commonly, if the supervisor cannot discuss such subjects comfortably because of personal experience or bias, he or she is likely to send the couple to another supervisor, friend, or company counselor.

I asked Jeanne Driscoll whether she thought the supervisor

should give in to lowered morale caused by gossip if two people are having an affair but are doing their jobs properly. "I don't think companies can get into that," she advised, "and say it is right or wrong. They need to tell the couple there is gossip. But they also need to tell the gossipers that the couple are doing their jobs. People may be prejudiced against their behavior but the supervisor should say, 'I'm sorry, you may believe whatever you care to believe, but on the job you are going to have to work with these people.' You don't tell the couple to 'cut it out—you are upsetting people.' You go to those people and say, 'It's not your business. As long as their personal relationship is kept at home, and they are doing their jobs, then you others will have to deal with your own feelings about it.' Otherwise," says Driscoll, "you can be held hostage to anybody. If the manager disapproves, he or she should manage himself on this issue."

Consultant and social psychologist Dr. Jennifer Macleod advises supervisors to approach the situation by assessing whether or not the couple's job performance is adversely affected. "You don't go at the affair head-on, because that's not anybody's business but their own."

An executive agreed. "That's the person's private business. I don't think people give up their civil rights, or should, when they walk in the door of the company. They should still have their privacy. All the company has a right to talk about is their performance on the job. And that goes for alcoholism or anything else." Though this advice will work well in a company that acknowledges the individual's privacy, it doesn't work everywhere. As we have seen, companies are capable of attacking an employee's private life directly, though often they will cover their tracks by circling around what is really bothering them and look for work-related problems, even creating them if necessary, to get rid of their amorous employees.

A high-level supervisor in advertising said a number of people had worked for him who have had affairs. He usually lets both people know he is aware of it, but makes no judgment on it. "I just request that it not in any way interfere with their work, which I think is fair. I call them into my office individually and tell them this. It's up to them, then, to make it happen."

He gave an example of how he solved a problem that arose when two people had an affair in his office and did not manage it well. It involved a married senior account executive and the female head of the art department, who was living with someone else. They often traveled together, but it seemed to the supervisor that an inordinate number of trips were being scheduled. In his opinion, neither was functioning at an optimum level of ability.

"I resented the fact, not that they could travel together," he said, "but that they were spending time away from the office when they didn't have to. I have no problem with people having affairs. I have a problem with people not doing their job to the height of their potential." One thing that bothered him was that the couple would schedule shootings in the Midwest or Florida when they could just as easily have scheduled them closer.

"I was fairly close to both people, since I'd worked with them intimately for a number of years. Now he was ready to do in his marriage. I called him in and asked him if he thought the whole thing was worth it. I guess he thought it was. Eventually, I had to move him to another account group so the two of them did not work together."

Despite what he did, this executive, like others, feels the best answer for any supervisor is to let the lovers themselves come up with a solution. "If they don't work it out, and it's still disruptive to the organization, then that doesn't leave you an option. You say, 'These are the ground rules. Here's what we pay each of you to do your work. If you can't handle that, you're going to leave us no option.' If they are talented people and you don't want to lose them, you transfer them, separate them as much as possible."

In transferring or firing employees, supervisors should be warned that they have to proceed with caution so that what is an attempt to avoid office disruption does not backfire and become an even more disruptive situation if the employee feels discriminated against and decides to sue. An advisor for the Equal Employment Opportunity Commission cautions that you cannot always fire only the woman and do nothing to the man or "you are buying liability under Title VII of the Civil Rights Act of 1964." Also, you must be consistent. Let's say a significant officer is having an affair with a woman who is a subordinate and the company wants to do something about it. The first thing she would advise them is, "Don't fire the woman. Find out what the company has done in the past. If the company has known of other affairs and done nothing, then they are stuck with this one."

If in the past both people have been fired because of a romantic liaison, then the company would have to fire both parties again, "because the issue is not having affairs as much as it is sex discrimination under Title VII." Then she advises supervisors to ask why the affair is so troubling. "If [the issue] is being raised, there must be reasons, and you want to deal with those reasons, not the affair."

If you transfer or fire one or both, you must be careful that you won't be accused of a "constructive" demotion or a "constructive" discharge. The person, in other words, can complain that the new job is not of equal status, or that you forced a resignation because you offered an intolerable alternative, which was the case with IBM and Gina Rulon-Miller. There is also the danger of being sued for wrongful discharge, as in the case of Slohoda and United Parcel.

Working up the right strategy to deal with a corporate romance is not easy. Lacking training in this field, the supervisor must use his or her own good judgment while trying to solve whatever problem has been created without imposing any personal morality, giving in to slanderous gossip, or incurring a legal suit. Due consideration must also be given to the norms of the particular corporate culture, which the supervisor may decide to ignore, obey, or try to change. Supervising may be one of the most difficult jobs in business today because of the range of problems that must be addressed, from personal human enigmas to the technical riddles of production. Corporations would certainly ease their managers' burdens if they offered them some special training in solving the human conundrums that exist in corporate society.

## *HBR* SPEAKS

The *Harvard Business Review* is the bible of business-school journals. It is universally quoted and its views are quickly absorbed into corporate attitudes. Therefore, it was particularly surprising and upsetting to read, in the September/October 1983 issue, an article on office romance called "Managers and Lovers," by Eliza G. C. Collins, an *HBR* senior editor. Stated simply, her conclusions were:

- A love affair between two executives should be treated as a conflict of interest. (She assumes that the executives would be competing for the same resources and power, and the departments they supervise would conflict. This could conceivably, but not necessarily, be the case. Even if it were, what's wrong with competition between friends and lovers? It happens among men in business, and it happens on the tennis court.)
- The manager should advise the couple to get outside help. (Her reason is that executives may not trust their boss's assessment of the situation because he is a member of the organization. If they don't trust their boss's judgment, they probably can't work well together on any matter. The boss should tackle his subordinates' problem with the help of the company counselors. After having said that bosses should stay out of it, the article concludes with an apparent contradiction, saying top

198

managers have to deal with these situations. Does the author mean deal with them by sending employees outside the company?)

· The couple should be persuaded that the person less essential to the company, usually the woman, has to leave. "Coming to the recognition that someone must go is painful but, I regret to say, inevitable. . . . Though I arrived at it with great reluctance, the conclusion is inescapable. . . . Managers need to believe in the inevitability of this outcome because they will have to counter endless entreaties and pleas for fairness." (Elsewhere in this article, the author writes: "Executives will need new ways to think about this phenomenon; neither the old sex-laden concepts nor simplistic policies will apply to what is already occurring and will continue to occur in organizations." Thus, having said that simpleminded policies won't work and new ones are needed, the author proceeds to a sexist, simpleminded conclusion—*fire the woman.*)

· She also says that in certain situations the man will be caught between loyalty to his company and to the woman he loves, and he will lose not only a sense of control but also his view of himself as the protector. (Do Harvard Business School women look upon their male colleagues as protectors? Does any business-school woman? Does any working woman? Several times editor Collins refers to love and sex as those "messy" human problems.)

Columnist Ellen Goodman, writing in *The Boston Globe,* said she found Collins' generalizations and recommendations "somewhere between offensive and dangerous." She called the tone of the article dangerous because it makes it seem as though women are bringing messy problems into business and male executives are all running around out of control, unable to function rationally at work.

Says Goodman, "The reality is that there are all sorts of special relationships between executives, all sorts of political and personal alliances in the corporate power structure that are untinged by sex." What Goodman finds so unsettling is that "once again, the business world is being fed the illusion that they can and, indeed, should manage emotions by removing them from the workplace. The prime candidate for emotional excision is, as always, love: first family love and, now, sexual love. . . . We go back again to the notion that a healthy business personality is different from a healthy human personality."

Aside from Collins' amazingly sexist solutions, her attitude toward human attraction and love is even more curious. Goodman quoted her in an interview as having said, "If the company sees rats in the basement, they've got to get them out." Collins apparently believes that since the company doesn't know how to handle such things as ratty romance, they should just get rid of it. If that is *HBR*'s latest intelligence on human resource management, one shudders for both executives and business.

A number of people were horrified by *HBR*'s advice. In a letter to the editor, Robert Schrank, visiting professor, Cornell University, said he was troubled by the opinions expressed, and that both love and work are essential for a well-adjusted, mature existence. He was appalled at the suggestion that women would have to leave. "This seems like a reversion to the medieval notion that the woman in an affair is a harlot, an adultress, a seducer, while the man is just having a little fun. I hope we are not reinventing that." He thinks it is no one's business except that of those in love. Otherwise we will have to have "love hunts" the way we once had witch hunts. Certainly the behavior of the managers at Foote & Davies described earlier was exactly that—a "love hunt" in which creative, productive employees were harassed simply because they were in love.

My advice to all managers who read *HBR*'s advice is to forget it! Not only is business confused about how to handle corporate romance, but business journals such as *HBR* don't know how to inform them on the subject either. Instead of useful insight, they offer sexist platitudes. Businesses should recognize that more imaginative, creative solutions exist for these situations; otherwise they will waste a lot of time and money firing some of their best people, and will construct a climate of suspicion and malicious gossip where mere rumor is enough to kill a career and where those who are power-hungry will spend their time manufacturing false information to get rid of any human obstacles in their path.

Offices could turn into places of fear and employees would be reduced to timid, apprehensive creatures, afraid a mere smile at a co-worker would be misunderstood and reported. Inventive ideas that normally evolve from an adult working environment would not be forthcoming. Male and female business colleagues would no longer be able to work or travel together; the practice of cross-sex mentors and protégés would die out. In fact, the only women who could survive in such a tense atmosphere would be token, sexless automatons. Business would be the loser—and business doesn't like to lose.

Innovation and insight is what business should be talking about. As long as there are women in executive positions, with more coming through the pipeline every day, it is time. One needn't wait for any magic percentage of women before following good business practices.

## SHOULD THERE BE RULES AT ALL?

Corporations, as we have seen, have gradually done away with their more restrictive rules, and even nepotism rules are now being challenged in the courts. Certainly there is a legitimate question about conflict of interest and favoritism, but it is no more crucial than it always has been. Favoritism and conflict of interest are not gender related, they are people related, and who says what to whom is probably more a function, not of one's sexual connection, but of one's own personal code of ethics. It is also a function of how much love and loyalty the corporation, through its policies and goals, has been able to instill. You cannot inspire loyalty through rules. They always exist as a challenge to be broken, especially when they make no sense.

Business should insist on a code of honesty, propriety, and productivity. Conflict of interest and favoritism seem impossible to control; they are occupational hazards, and to focus attention on them only in the cross-sex arena and not in the same-sex arena is grossly discriminatory.

Obviously if two lovers are granting each other special favors, the corporation could step in on the grounds that they are not doing their jobs in an honorable manner. Job failure rather than the sexual relationship should be the cause for concern, and helping those involved to overcome the lapse in productivity should also be the company's responsibility.

If the corporation feels it cannot trust its employees to act like adults or if it wishes to remind them of certain guidelines, it should spell them out clearly, make them known to everyone, and enforce them equally among men and women. If they are not discriminatory (the discriminatory ones usually remain unwritten) and cannot be challenged in the courts, then it is up to each employee to decide whether or not he or she wants to work in such a place.

The need for confidentiality, which we are warned ad nauseam will be breached by "pillow talk," does exist. However, I can't help wondering how much business is actually so confidential that employees within the same company ought not know about it or be able to discuss it freely. If employees care at all about their company's success, they are not going to repeat anything that would knife their corporation in the back. Are a lot of fuss and firings taking place over nothing? To think that dispatching the lowly woman in a case of love, or writing a list of innocuous rules, will do away with favoritism and conflict of interest, or placate the demands for confidentiality, is ludicrous. Besides, many situations exist where couples successfully keep information from each other because of their code of ethics—doctors, diplomats, and the military come to mind. There are the daily white lies we all tell or the things we don't mention to our spouses, in order not to make waves.

How do the executives themselves feel about the monitoring of corporate romance? One manager commented that the company should allow affairs. "It all boils down to 'Even if married people are having affairs, am I doing the job I was hired to do?' "

Another executive came out against all romantic rules. He replied, "Baloney! You should never have a policy that you can't implement. There's no way any corporation could do this."

"Large corporations end up setting hard-and-fast guidelines for everything, and people just don't fit into them," said a vice president. "No situation ever exactly fits the guidelines, so it's difficult to deal with people if these are the corporate ethics you have to enforce. So you end up going around them. Almost every good manager will do that. Go around or overlook them."

A human-resources vice president said, "The corporation should stop firing people or pressuring them to leave. It's up to the two of them. I know of a guy who was general counsel and the woman was the controller. They were having an affair, and the man left, which shook up the organization. He left because one of the two *had* to leave. They were both senior officers, and it was company policy. I think the policy is outdated," he said. "There might be some reason for confidentiality, but I can't think of one. The policy should probably be looked at and looked at hard. Legally, they don't have to fire anyone. Lots of companies have husband-wife teams, for example. It's up to the corporation."

One executive whose company has no such rules, not even

against nepotism, said that whatever message is conveyed comes not so much from rules, but from the top. "It's important that upper management conduct itself in an exemplary way to set the tone for the company. If you've got presidents and vice presidents playing around with the help, that's going to be the tone."

And Frederic Withington, vice president of Arthur D. Little, one of the few executives who allowed me to use his name, said, "I think the corporation should stay out of it. It should be very simple. What you do with your emotional affairs is none of our business unless your productivity drops off to the point where you are no longer a useful employee—at which point we reserve the right to fire you. And if the affair appears to be in the way, a fatherly word to the wise might be advisable."

Dr. Terence McGuire, psychiatrist, doesn't think the corporation should have any cut-and-dried rules about relations but should deal with each case individually. "The more you make rules," he counsels, "the more they hem you in every bit as much as they help you." When he was an administrator in a hospital, he had thousands of people working for him. "You may promulgate a rule meant to control a handful of bad folks—bad meaning they are not functioning as the rest feel they should—and that rule may make many problems for you.

"At times it is best just to say, 'We expect reasonable behavior in our company,' and occasionally define what is reasonable for an individual—although most of the people would have arrived at that conclusion without your having to tell them.

"If you make a rule," he points out, "about a third of the population don't need the rule in the first place because they never would have done whatever the rule prohibits; there's another third that might be deterred by the rule; and there's roughly another third that finds it a challenge, and they'll try and find some way around it. So when you make rules, you have to use a little discretion about it," he cautions. "With all the different kinds of people there are, you need to leave yourself lots of flexibility."

Certainly the more rules there are, the more there are to break and create problems that otherwise might not exist. Rules appear to be phasing out because corporations can't withstand the legal challenges. Ideally, the fewer rules—and the greater self-generated loyalty—the better.

## CURRENT CORPORATE RESPONSE

In Professor Robert E. Quinn's "Cupid" study, which was discussed earlier, businessmen and businesswomen were asked how the superiors handled the affairs they reported. According to the study, the superiors ignored the romance in 60 percent of the cases. Fifty-two percent thought the problem would resolve itself, 39 percent did not want to risk any action, and as many as 36 percent did not know what to do. It seems extraordinary that over a third of the supervisors, whose job it is to handle such situations, found themselves totally at sea.

In cases where the supervisor took punitive action, the male's superior reprimanded him in 12 percent of the romances, but the female's supervisor reprimanded her in only 6 percent of the cases. Employees were warned in 10 percent of the instances, and transferred in 6 percent. Women were fired twice as often as men, 10 percent compared with 5 percent, but obviously very few were fired.

In terms of taking some positive action, one third of the males' superiors openly discussed the situation with the couple, but a surprisingly low percentage, only 6 percent, of the females' supervisors spoke to the woman involved, probably because the supervisors were men and they would find talking to women about such subjects difficult and awkward. Some, in fact, said they found it embarrassing to have to tell their subordinates that their personal lives were out of control and would have to change. Managers were also hesitant to initiate such a discussion with either sex because, as one said, "If the guy denies that a relationship exists, what do you say then?" It was often thought the situation would resolve itself because either one might be scheduled for a transfer, or the affair would soon be over.

In the study of executives' attitudes toward romance done by BFS Psychological Associates of New York, one of the questions businessmen were asked was, "Do you believe in a policy of absolute hands off in cases of simple romance?" Fifty-one percent said yes, 35 percent said no, and 14 percent avoided any answer.

But when asked how they felt when it came to "more complex relationships," only 29 percent in this study said "hands off" and the majority, or 55 percent, said they thought the company should intervene. Seventeen percent refused to answer the question. The authors of this study, Mortimer Feinberg and Aaron Levenstein, reported that 68 percent of the people involved in a sexual relationship had been admonished by their superiors to observe caution; 45 percent said warnings were issued to discontinue the relationship. And in some instances, the relationship was penalized by a denial of promotion or by some other action, such as firing the person involved. However, most respondents said that discussion between a supervisor and the couple usually led to resignation rather than discharge.

The Quinn study showed that the majority of supervisors tried to ignore the romance, while in the BFS study the majority thought, in the case of complex situations, that the corporation should become involved. One reason for the discrepancy in attitudes may be the difference in questionnaires. The BFS study differentiates between simple and more serious relationships, and the Quinn study does not. Another reason may be that BFS conducted their study through the mail, allowing more time for thought in responding, while Quinn's study was done verbally in busy airports. Also, Quinn's study was reported on in 1977, and the questionnaires were actually completed in 1976, while BFS did theirs seven years later, in 1983. Views are changing that quickly. In addition, the BFS study may have included more high-level executives. Neither study can be called definitive.

To find out more specifically what current executive thinking is on how to respond to office romances, I culled the following unpublished comments from the BFS study, to which the authors kindly gave me access. The executives describe what *is* being done, and not always what should be done. My own judgment of their action appears in parentheses.

- According to one president, policies are too complex for rigidity. He favored hands off. (If possible, this is the best solution.)
- The CEO of a large health-care company said, "If either party is married to someone else, I think management must take action," He would force the resignation of both people. (This is making a moral judgment about these people's personal lives.)
- Another president reported an affair between his manager and a woman employee which caused personal problems at home and negatively affected the manager's job performance. The company sent the manager and his wife to a transactional analyst. (Paying for professional help, in addition to whatever advice the boss can give, makes sense. The couple can examine their marriage and find out if they want it to continue, and the manager will be able to judge what he wants to do about his affair. With such personal problems solved, performance should shoot back up to normal.)
- A senior VP in a corporation of 40,000 reported that a corporate executive who was playing around was told to quit, or else! (If he was doing his job and not interfering with others doing their jobs, he should have been

left alone, unless he publicly embarrassed the company.)

- In another case at this corporation, two employees in the same department who were having a romance were told that one would have to go elsewhere in the company or find another job. Said the senior VP, "Dealing with problems fairly, competently, and objectively is tough!" (I think it is unfortunate to respond in this automatic way. We are not given enough facts to make an exact judgment, but it could be that both people might have done a super job if left in the same department.)
- The chairman of the board of a corporation with 3,000 employees said he had no concern about singles, but was very worried about married people philandering. He felt it was damaging to the company, and pressure was applied to get those concerned to stop. (If the company is in a very conservative geographic pocket, it could be that gossip about marriages being broken up would hurt local business. It is also true that employees who feel defensive about marriage, and have shaky unions themselves, resent seeing married people playing around. However, one cannot monitor married couples as though they were children. The chairman should not be the one to decide whether married people should date others.)
- The vice president of a company of 1,800 said that in some cases he thought a romantic relationship "provides stability if handled well." (Three cheers for him!)
- The president of an aerospace company said in one case the "action" was going on on the premises. "This is a real no-no." (He is absolutely right.)
- A director of human resources in a manufacturing company of 16,000 employees reported that two individuals in two different departments began to meet at times

and in places that might have had a negative impact on their productivity. Each person was counseled separately. The company position was that it was not interested in becoming involved with their personal affairs; however, it *was* concerned with job performance. After being counseled, but not by the immediate superior, the employees used more discretion. (The company handled a potential problem intelligently. I presume they felt that if the counseling came from someone besides the immediate supervisor, everyone would be able to work better. Ideally, the supervisor should be able to handle the matter without its interfering with their mutual trust, but such is not always the case.)

- A corporation officer suggested placing people on probation for six months and then discharging them if it continued. "Business life must be kept on an impersonal basis." (Was job performance affected? The officer doesn't say. If it was, then sometimes people need time to get back on the track. But the notion of a probation period smacks of a prison mentality.)

- A senior vice president of a banking company said he thought legitimate romances caused no problems. "An occasional 'Lothario' or 'Bitch' has caused problems." But he pointed out that usually an ill-behaved person has other drawbacks, too. (I couldn't agree more, and these other problems will be the person's downfall.)

- A district manager of a publishing company knew of many romances and complained that stories get distorted, and too much time is wasted either spreading gossip or defending the participants. (It would be far wiser if supervisors chastised the scandalmongers for a change, instead of their targets, the majority of whom are probably doing their jobs despite any real—or imagined—romances.)

209

# CORPORATE ROMANCE

## <u>A WORD FROM THE EXPERTS</u>

I have discussed various kinds of problems and their possible solutions, but basically I think corporations should consider the issue of corporate romance in creative terms, rather than grabbing at some cookie-cutter solution. What works for a provincial company in Nebraska may not work for a multinational corporation in New York. What makes sense for a small company may not work in a large one. But there are certain freedoms that belong in every organization.

Consultant Kaleel Jamison says the critical thing for any corporation is that it become more aware of the dynamics of man-woman work relationships, and that it understand the sexist stereotypes we have carried around with us for so many years.

Second, companies must acquire the skills men and women need to work together. Part of that would include learning how to deal with both sexual attraction and sexual harassment. "In many organizations," she explained, "employees are so frightened that they don't understand the difference between attraction and harassment. In cases where attraction can be well managed, the company should be supportive because I think it can enhance productivity."

Companies are *not* supportive these days, says Jamison, when they ship one of the couple to "Siberia" or fire someone as soon as they find out what's going on. Nor are they supportive if they make the assumption that because two people are in love, there is no room for those feelings at work. In her opinion, the corporation should define for itself the relationships it feels are disruptive.

Since one might assume that the more attractive men and women are the ones who most easily become involved in sexual imbroglios, I asked Harvard Business School professor Laura Nash if she thought that in the future, it might come to the point where

Personnel would surreptitiously begin to hire only the ugly duck-lings, immediately discarding anyone who looked the least bit sexually attractive.

"That certainly is not going to happen. Surveys show that attractive people tend to get hired and promoted more easily," she said. "I don't think that is going to change. But I do think what business can do to ease things is in the training, the writing up of a clear rule book, having open discussions and seminars. That way the reasons for any rule they have can get community-wide acceptance. If a business relies on discretionary behavior, what so often happens is you get this cut-and-dried rule that has no shared meaning in terms of how to apply it. What gives a code of conduct meaning is to begin to apply it and explore it as a group. You need to understand how the group perceives it, be-cause individually we may see things very differently. I'm all for a lot of time spent on management self-examination." She said she thought corporations have an obligation to facilitate that, and added that the outcome would be in their own self-interest.

Consultant Nancy Brown of Cincinnati also feels that corpora-tions should legitimize sexual attraction and it should be the subject of work-related discussion, so people feel free to raise these issues when they need to. "I don't think an increase in women in the corporation means that sexual attraction will become easier to talk about. I think there has to be some conscious effort to make that happen, so that people can develop a personal ethic."

Brown feels women and men can manage their mutual attrac-tions and enjoy them without letting them get in the way of work, particularly if they choose to acknowledge them verbally, without necessarily acting on them. She would like to see a corporate climate where it is okay to say to someone of the opposite sex, "You really look terrific today," or, "That's a smashing suit you have on," or even to say in a close working relationship, "You know, Jack, I've really been attracted to you. I think you are a really neat person to work with. I don't want to make anything of that but I don't want to deny it either. I want to enjoy it as well as the other parts of the relationship we have working with each other."

Working in an environment that encourages employees to say such things would help couples manage an attraction when they choose *not* to act on it. "It's much easier if I have some outlet for articulating that side of me," Brown said. The innovative corporation will have awareness sessions or other discussion groups which would make it possible for people to discuss their normal sexual attractions with each other in order to discharge the electricity verbally.

For example, consultant Janice Eddy runs a seminar in her home in Maine where executives from the few unusual companies who care may come and tackle such subjects. Recently a meeting of top male and female executives from a high-tech company took place where both men and women tried to learn how to be more interdependent, to know more about each other personally, and to be closer friends at work.

This remarkably enlightened company believes, says Eddy, "that if these people really care more about one another as individual human beings, if they get beyond whatever barriers there are, black-white, male-female, and reach that kind of interdependence, the company is going to profit."

It would seem logical that as corporations hire and promote more women executives, they should work to lessen confusion, resentment, rivalries, and competition. Then, coupled with the essential open discussion groups—larger numbers of women alone will probably not do the whole job of budging people out of their long-ingrained attitudes—there is hope of creating a more normal ambiance where sexual tensions, preconceptions, stereotypes, and assumptions evaporate, the cross-sex barriers are broken down, and men and women are free to do their best work. This, too, should put a damper on the need to gossip. And in this process the older working generation will catch on to what business—with the new generation of men and women working together naturally, as friends and equal colleagues—is going to be all about.

# Chapter 8

# TOWARD A NEW CORPORATE POLICY

$\mathscr{A}$s we have seen, corporate policies are in a serious state of transition. Accepting woman was the first big hurdle for business. Understanding them and relating to them is the next.

In 1974, a study conducted by Opinion Research Corporation found that 75 percent of the executives representing the nation's largest businesses believed that women were discriminated against. In the current survey done in 1982, 530 top- and middle-management people were sampled from the largest manufacturing, banking, utilities, transportation, merchandising, life insurance, and diversified finance companies. The results show a dramatic change. Only 53 percent thought that women were discriminated against. The most frequent practices cited were the lack of equal opportunity to grow and the failure to promote women to management positions. Merchandising and banking were the least discriminatory, while manufacturing was the most.

To the question of why women were discriminated against, the major reasons given were "tradition" and "prejudice." Interestingly, 77 percent of the executives who acknowledged this discrimination said they felt such reasons were not valid. Almost all the executives queried believed this sex bias would eventually disappear because women would be recognized as career-minded and capable, and attitudes toward the traditional roles of women would change.

There is not doubt that men are having difficulty seeing women in their new executive roles. One can document the psychological reactions we experience toward people when they are in the

214

minority or are the only ones of their kind in a group. Researchers call these people "solos."

Shelley E. Taylor, a psychology professor at UCLA, and her colleagues studied situations similar to those present in today's executive offices. They were able to simulate groups with various male-female ratios by playing a tape of a discussion while showing slides of people talking. By changing the voices and pictures, they could manipulate the sex composition of the group without changing the actual discussion.

Some subjects in the test saw a group of six men, some saw an integrated group of three men and three women, and some saw a group of one woman and five men—the "token" or "solo" condition, which is often found in business.

Subjects were asked to rate each of the six participants as to how much the person had influenced the conversation, was liked by the other participants, was respected by the others, and had talked. Subjects were also asked how competent and interesting the person was, and the extent to which they formed a clear impression of him or her.

An analysis of the results showed a consistent and strong pattern indicating that a solo person, whether female or male, is regarded as a more prominent group member, talking more, making a stronger impression, having a stronger personality, being more confident, assertive, and individualistic than the same individual in a mixed group.

Also, a special role was attributed to the solo more often than to the same person in a mixed group. The characteristics of the role were also stereotyped, with 25 percent of them having sexual connotations, such as "She's the motherly type," "a secretary type," or "a bitch." However, in mixed-group situations, only half as many, or 13 percent, of the roles were sex typed. It was also found that the solo is likely to be sensitive to group members' reactions and that his or her behavior will mirror the group's expectations.

What this all means, according to Professor Taylor, is that solos, or in this case women in business, are evaluated more extremely than men in a positive or negative way. They are more likely to be cast in stereotyped roles, and because the solo is novel in the environment, a disproportionate amount of attention is directed to her. It is not possible for her to fade into the background. She is conspicuous even when not talking. She cannot tell a bad joke because it will hang around longer than when a man tells one. The woman is watched, noticed, and monitored a disproportionate amount of the time. People focus their attention on her. And thus it is harder for her to have an affair without people guessing.

Considering that the sexual exploits of executives everywhere have caused problems and attracted attention, it should be extremely unnerving for corporate officers to realize that, as the number of executive women increases, the male-female difficulties should also increase alarmingly until some magic number is reached. Yale sociologist Dr. Rosabeth Kanter, for example, thinks it will happen when 35 percent of the workers in any group are women. Dr. Taylor's research appears to show that although people still think in stereotypic terms, the inclination to do so lessens when the sexes are more equal in numbers. At the moment, women are in a no-man's-land. There are some, but not enough of them; they are included, but not equally included.

The extent of their discomfort was demonstrated in a 1984 *Wall Street Journal*/Gallup Survey of 722 women executives with the title of vice president or higher in companies with annual sales of $100 million or more. In telephone interviews conducted by other women, these executives said that being women affects their job performance in several ways. Sixty percent had the impression that their views were not respected as much as a man's in certain areas, 37 percent felt they were being judged more on the basis of dress than a man would be, 29 percent felt their personal lives were being scrutinized more than those of their male colleagues, and 24 percent felt uncomfortable about socializing with a male colleague because it would not look right. During this transition period things are awkward for women. One reason is that men are so accustomed to the cliché of what a woman is that they cannot accept her fully in her new role. And the woman may not be able to accept herself fully in that role, either.

One professor reported that his women students do not participate as much in class as the male students. "They seem to feel that if they were to speak out on a professional issue, their sexuality would be compromised, they would appear to be behaving like men, and their social interactions with peers in that class—the same feeling that goes into the business community—would be compromised. They would rather be viewed as women who are passive and therefore more acceptable to men."

Thus women appear to be operating on a split level where the two needs and ambitions conflict, a rather paralyzing state for anyone. They want to be accepted by the business world, yet they want to remain women and remain attractive to men, and they fear the two are not compatible. That a man is not capable of accepting sexually a woman who is not passive, who realizes her potential in many ways, is probably a male myth. Women, too, also operate with myths about men. How long will it take for the stereotypes to disappear? Until a decade ago, there were very few women in business schools and almost no women in business. Now there are some women at the top and lots of women in middle management. That has taken ten years. That's progress. But it will probably be another twenty or thirty years before women reach the next stage. They have been raised by conventional men and women who have gone through this tremendous social change, but they are not yet that different.

This was dramatically observed in a survey by Dr. Peter Dubno, professor of behavioral science and management at New York University Graduate School of Business Administration. Students from three graduate schools of business were surveyed in 1975,

1978, and 1983, and despite the feminist movement, the drive for the Equal Rights Amendment, and the increase in number of women in business schools, the majority of male business students continue to feel negative about women as managers. There was no change in attitude over the eight-year period, much to Professor Dubno's surprise. The male students queried do not believe women should be in decision-making positions, though they were not asked why. Ironically, NYU Business School now has a higher percent of women students than men.

## TURNING THINGS AROUND

Though the major changes that will happen will require another generation at least, amazing changes have already taken place. There are now organizations in which men may take paternity leave without being penalized in any way, a total impossibility a few years ago. And a 1980 Roper Poll reported that two thirds of all working men and women said it mades no difference to them whether they had a male or a female boss.

Moving women higher up in management has begun to change attitudes. An executive in an international corporation who was recently promoted tells about working with men who usually make a habit of ignoring women. "You are nobody. They don't even see you," she says. "Then I became a director, and men who had known who I was for years, but didn't see me, suddenly changed. Now I walk into a meeting and it's 'Hello Mary, how are you? It's good to see you.'" She says one man in her department now acts as though she were one of the boys. His attitude has changed dramatically, as has that of other vice presidents.

As women stumble through the transition stage, some try to pattern themselves after men, others try to hold on to their femininity, and many waver, not knowing which attitude is right. It is to be hoped that as they rise in numbers in the hierarchy, they will, as Cincinnati management consultant Nancy Brown says, "hang on to their sense of themselves as whole human beings, including their intelligence, their creativity, their spontaneity, their sexuality, and they will thus, in a sense, be models for men, proving that it is possible to be whole in an organization, and to be successful."

If women are allowed to be whole people, with their emotions and sexuality as well as their business sense intact, their normal adult interactions with men who can understand them should, I think, be interesting for marriages of the future. As a director of human resources put it, "I think there are going to be some exciting relationships. You are building this interaction around using your brain, your emotions, your romance, and both individuals will feel they are contributing to society with their work, not just through family and children."

There are also signs of a turnaround in male behavior. One avenue of reeducation is the fact that many male corporate executives have daughters who are entering the work force, and who bring home the new realities. These fathers are supporting their daughters' business education, helping them get jobs, and rooting for them to succeed. It's got to have some impact.

Philip Sardella, a manager at a high-tech corporation, who says he sees the male-female issue "not just coming up in my company, it's all over the place," also senses the beginnings of a shift in the corporate value structure. "Men are seeing that the approaches they traditionally used in relating to women don't work anymore. Women now don't want to be related to in that same way. And men are becoming aware that the traditional male values are not necessarily the ones that are important anymore."

As Sardella points out, "the big macho decision-maker is not what is needed for success in business. Today it is teamwork, nurturing, and networking that get creative results. Men are learning that they need to listen to what women are saying, and not just react. They are learning they must give women air time and not clog the conversation, that they don't need to be the center of attention all the time, simply because they are men. They are learning that they must have a process that includes both women and men in the decision-making."

He believes one thing that impedes more rapid change is the whole societal notion of what is a man. "Society paints the picture of the man being very strong and knowing it all, having all the answers," says Sardella, "when the reality is, this is probably not true. I think a lot of men have been bamboozled into thinking that's the way we had to be when, in fact, that is probably not the way. That idea was programmed into us. You know, little boys are still told that they should not cry. It's still there." Sardella would like to see people get beyond the male-female issues to the human issues that are generic to both groups.

## A NEW BREED OF EXECUTIVE

There is no question about the difference between the present breed of young men and women and the older men at the top whom they will eventually replace. Some of the older men may have their consciousness raised by their wives and daughters, but they have not experienced the same rapport with women in all facets of their lives. They have not had any experience working with women in an equal, collaborative relationship. Despite Professor Dubno's survey showing that young males still have trouble accepting the notion of women as managers (are they hoping to save the best job offers for themselves?), young men today simply relate differently to women, and both sexes bring fresh expectations into the corporation. If the organization is to have well-adjusted, productive executives, these new expectations must be respected.

For example, there is a growing resistance among young executives to relocating when the company wants people to move, because their wives, husbands, or special friends also have difficulty switching. Dr. Meredith Titus of the Menninger Foundation says one of the main stresses she sees among young executives is a recognition that although they have always wanted to work full-out toward their ambitions and goals, they sense a growing awareness of the need their children have for them, or their need to be more connected to their children's lives. They also want to know how to have a gratifying, equal relationship with their spouses, in which they can share all the home responsibilities and still do what the corporation demands of them. "Often they feel that what makes them a good father or husband," said Titus, "isn't consistent with what would make them a good employee." People are becoming more interested in the quality of their lives, and just as women are willing to become superwomen, men seem also to want it all. "They want to feel good about themselves as father and husband, and also as a successful career person."

A director of human resources for a leading corporation has noticed the stirrings of change. "Young people coming in have different value sets than we do, and top management will have to adapt to those values. Their assumptions of what are "musts" on the job are very different from ours. Their whole lifestyle trade-offs are different, and they are not going to work long hours and relocate from one place to another. And they are going to take their vacations and not skip them. They have had affairs in college and will expect to continue to. If top management doesn't adapt to that," said this director, "then they will run into problems all the way through. Companies will have to change their policies."

A vice president also noted, "Younger people's attitudes are different. Work is a part of life, but men and women both feel the company should make room for their family responsibilities. Young executives worry about this."

A young manager said, "If I couldn't fraternize, it would make me question a lot of the policies of the organization. Is it attempting to control my destiny or my life too much?" From a career standpoint, that is important to him. He said he and his young wife, also an executive, have talked about this. "Where are your priorities? What comes first, the corporation, or your private life and marriage? And I have to say," he continued with stern conviction, "if I make a commitment to my job, then I'll be there by eight-thirty and I won't leave till six, and they are going to see me there. But let me hear that my wife has a problem, then I don't care if I've scheduled the most important meeting of my career, I'm going to fix up the problem first. My company will know that!"

In a class at the University of Virginia's Darden Graduate School of Business Administration, the presiding professor asked his students whether they thought it was appropriate, considering the sexual freedom among males and females in business, to "fish off the company pier." There was a divergence of opinion. Some said, "Never." Some said, "I'm not going to let the company keep me from pursuing a good relationship." And one fellow said, "There's no question for me. I'd take a hundred different jobs in order to maintain one good relationship." Everyone applauded.

In September 1983, Harvard University issued a report on a survey they had conducted of sexual harassment. The survey queried the Arts and Sciences faculty of 700, plus 1,000 graduate students and 2,000 undergraduates. Part of the questionnaire concerned "relationships between consenting parties." Although faculty responses were included, it is interesting to see what a preponderance of younger people and a full complement of thinking people felt about who should be able to have affairs and when.

Asked about affairs between a student and a professor with direct authority over that student (the business equivalent would be a supervisor and someone reporting to him or her), 80 percent considered such relationships to be always or usually inappropriate, with only 20 percent approving.

When the question was asked about professor-student romances where there was no direct authority of one over the other, the statistics dropped dramatically. Only 30 percent of the respondents said it is always or usually wrong, with 70 percent saying it is all right, and a mere 5 percent saying it is always wrong. In other words, the majority does not like to see a sexual relationship between people where one has authority or power over the other. When that is not the situation, they become extremely tolerant of affairs. This is somewhat surprising, because the prevailing attitude on campuses has been that *any* relationship between a professor and a student is completely off-limits.

## A SURVEY OF BUSINESS STUDENTS

To pinpoint the mood of rising MBAs concerning the subject of personal relationships, and to find out exactly how they can be expected to behave once they join an organization—how in fact attitudes have changed toward sexual interaction—I conducted my own survey of 70 male and female graduate business-school students. I also wanted to know what qualities of life are most important to them.

- "If you were a young executive, would you have an affair with another executive in your office, even if it were against company behavior guidelines?"
  61 percent said they would do it anyway.
- "If you decided to disobey the rules, would you then expect to be fired?"
  80 percent said they would not expect to be fired.
- "Would you perhaps expect to be transferred?"
  41 percent said they would expect to transfer and 46 percent said they would not.
  Obviously, a lot of them expect to be left alone even when disobeying guidelines they apparently would find difficult to accept. They might try to keep the affair secret, but most of them would go right ahead and have it.
- "If you both wanted the affair, would it stop you if one of you were married?"

80 percent of the students said it would.

Marriage to them is a commitment. This response agrees with those of young executives already in business who say they are not going to let their jobs destroy their personal lives.

- "How do you think the corporation should handle an affair among two of its executives—ignore it, warn the two to stop, fire the less important one, transfer one, discuss the problem with the couple, try to give the couple work to do as a team, or forbid affairs as disruptive and a conflict of interest? The overwhelming majority of students said, "Discuss the problem with the couple."

The second most often suggested solution was "Ignore it."

Firing the less important executive, which was the *Harvard Business Review*'s advice, was not supported by a single student.

Only 16 percent suggested transferring as the best solution. What this means is that if corporations plan to continue their current policy of firing and transferring, they are going to have a lot of angry young employees who will probably cause far more disruption in reaction to the policies than any affair would cause.

- "Is a corporate code of personal behavior possible to enforce?"

Half the students said no. Presumably it is up to each individual to form and live by his or her own code, but 35 percent thought such a code could be enforced.

However, when asked if they thought romance could be legislated, 70 percent of them said it could not. This indicates to me that most feel it is really going to be up to couples, in the final analysis, to make and live by their own sensible behavior guidelines, and that no company can control whether people have romantic involvements or not.

• "Suppose two executives are having an affair; do you think that decisions can be made fairly and objectively despite their romantic liaison?"

As many as 72 percent said yes. Apparently they do not see having an affair as so disorienting that the couple would be unable to think and act clearly.

When pressed further and asked if decisions could be made fairly and objectively if one reported to the other or influenced the other's career, 59 percent said no. Again, there is a consistent feeling among young people (and on this point alone they agree with their elders) that having an affair in a reporting relationship is too risky, though without a doubt some couples would be capable of it (that 41 percent?) and of being fair.

• "Suppose you do not report to each other, would you tell your lover in the same corporation, or a competing one, a secret to help him or her get ahead?"

Just where did their loyalties lie, primarily to the corporation or to their lover? One male student smartly replied, "She wouldn't ask me for it." Here we have a bit of a conflict. People are not unanimously sure which should come first in this hypothetical question. Their response showed that the majority, or 55 percent, said they would tell their lover a secret, but 41 percent said they would not. I imagine the circumstances would have a lot to do with their decision, and many could go either way, depending on whether the secret would damage the company.

• "What do you think is most important in your life of the following six choices: money, power, success, a good life, the love of another person, to fulfill yourself?"

In the recent past, this question would have elicited such answers as money, power, and success. They were what the efforts of our fathers were all about, what every young man wanted.

Now, over half the students, 54 percent, said that a good life—not money, power, or success—was most important to them. The second most often mentioned choice, 36 percent, was self-fulfillment. The third most frequently chosen requirement of life was the love of another person, which was mentioned by 20 percent of the students. Success was chosen as most important by only 16 percent, money by 10 percent, and power by only 2 percent.

## THE COUPLE TEAM

One of the innovative work styles that should be developed is the use of couple teams. With couples, married or not, working for the same companies, challenged by the same problems, it makes sense to allow them to work together rather than taking extraordinary measures to keep them apart, and then worrying about what they may tell each other. There are many lovers and married couples who would never want to spend all day and all evening together, and who would prefer the separation working apart gives them. But for others, it can be an exciting stimulus.

For example, in consulting, advertising, and sales, where a lot of travel is required and working with clients in various cities away from home is part of the life, I cannot think of anything more productive—if the couple wants it—than sending such teams out together. If the lovers are not married and sleep together, it is of no concern to the corporation. What the company can and should document is their productivity. Such synergistic mingling of work time, creative ideas, and energy should, in most cases, pay off. When it doesn't, when people take advantage of the company, their productivity will drop and they will be treated like any single person whose value is falling, for whatever reason. Many couples have worked together extremely productively in their own businesses, or for corporations such as Xerox in Rochester, New York, Southwestern Bell Telephone Company in Texas, and Merck & Company in Rahway, New Jersey. Couples throughout history have collaborated in scientific research, in literary, historical, and other projects. And there have been many collaborations where only the man received the credit for a job which could not have been done without the help of his wife.

There is no doubt that such a system would not suit everyone or every business. Many details would have to be tried and modified as people gain experience with them, such as whether the team would work best if both members were limited to perpetually having equal power.

One top-level executive wanted a newly married couple to work for him. They were both excellent workers and might have made a good team. He said he had no problem with the fact that they were married to each other. The couple turned down the offer because they felt the situation would introduce too many complications.

"Suppose we are in a group staff meeting and we have to take independent views on a controversial issue. If I sided with my wife then people would wonder, 'Is that just because they are married, or do they really feel that way?' Or if we disagreed, was it just a matter of marital strife?"

He said, "I'm no saint, and there's no way I could simplify things so much that I could separate the emotional side of our lives from the business side."

It may be that these two people should not work together as a team, or it may be that they have not grown up seeing couple teams in action.

I suggested this idea to a pair of lawyers, and here is their response:

**HE:** There would be a personality conflict if we worked together.

**SHE:** We both tend to be strong-willed, and we are perfectly able to curb it with people we work for, but we'd get more annoyed together because we just wouldn't restrain ourselves the way we would with others.

**HE:** People who love each other and enjoy living together cannot necessarily work together.

**SHE:** That's an awful lot of time to spend with one person. We both like work, and the time we spend together is important, but it's nice to have something that's entirely your own, that you feel you did yourself. The trouble with working closely with someone like that is that you don't have anything that's yours. You'd have in the back of your mind, did I do this because of his help? It's important to me to know when I'm doing well on my own.

For this couple, who both work for the same corporation, teamwork seems out of the question. Karen Brethower, psychologist and former director of manpower development at Chase Manhattan Bank, believes a couple's ups and downs are amplified when they operate as a team. She says such a work relationship "takes a level of skill, openness, and ability to handle conflict that most people are still neophytes at. But it *is* wonderful in the good times. It's fabulous and it's exciting. It's also equally awful in the bad times, and there's no escape."

Though still untested, teamwork, for the right couple, could be fantastic. It needs to be tried more often so that supervisors and couples can find out how to make it function. Brethower says, "I can imagine its working in the future. At some point all of this concern will just look silly and anachronistic. What you are talking about is, with whom do you collaborate most productively? And an aspect of that is going to be those people with whom you are really electric. They get your ideas going. They energize you.

But right now we've got big walls around it."

Social psychologist and consultant Dr. Jennifer Macleod believes that having men and women work as teammates, where they have to rely on each other in a purely professional way, is going to change the atmosphere in corporations. It will no longer be automatically assumed that a man and a woman who spend a lot of time together have a sexual relationship that interferes with work. Such bonds will be perceived as two-people relationships rather than as male-and-female. This can be a great advantage to the corporation in one sense because one of the big problems today for business is trying to transfer a member of a couple when one can't move or doesn't want to. If the two work as a team, the corporation has control over the situation and can see,to it that there is a job for both.

Dr. Macleod also envisions situations where one job could be shared by the couple, each working half the hours, and taking turns caring for the children.

The vice president of a consulting firm says his executives are sent out on the road continuously visiting with clients. "So if a husband-wife team can go out batting around, visiting the clients and doing professional work, and they both do a good job working together, if the clients find them satisfactory and pay their billing rates and are happy, why we'd be happy, too." He thought this arrangement might be easier than a line situation where promotion might be a function of favoritism.

In this case, the company could treat the two as a unit, promoting neither or both. If one member of the couple felt held back by the other, they could disband their team. In other words, corporate life would imitate real life in the sense that there would be singles and couples in several stages of romantic attachment, ranging from an affair to a marriage, all operating in the corporate society.

Menninger's Dr. Titus said she believes that if people had an affair and worked together they would probably "pick up steam, get very committed, and their relationship would become very intense, thus adding an enthusiasm to the job which would result in increased cooperation and productivity."

A director of a corporation also thought lovers working together could be an advantage to the company. "A lot of being able to do a job well," said this officer, "especially at a higher level, is to know what is going on. You have to know what other people are doing and how they are doing it. But there are a lot of executives who do not communicate with you because they feel threatened. They all try to cover themselves. So if you and your lover worked together and fed each other information, I think you could really do a super job for the corporation."

Another executive said he thought it might be a question of American corporate life growing up and getting used to having women in it, and having the husband and wife working in the same firm separately or together.

Walter Barlow, former president of Opinion Research Corporation and now president of Research Strategies Corporation of Princeton, New Jersey, says, "If a husband-and-wife team or liaison team working together in the same company can produce ideas, so that one plus one equals two and a half, then the smart companies will find a way to do it.

"In the smart companies that I work with," he continued, "and I work with a lot of them, I have watched the prejudice against women undergo remarkable change in the last ten years. If it can change that much in ten years, just look down the pike." He said if you have a situation where people can work pretty much on their own, then maybe a husband-and-wife team can work more effectively than two people working separately, "in which case I think the companies that recognize that will capitalize on it. Husband-and-wife sales teams, for example, could be a winning idea."

(It won't end there. To return to the political situation with which I started this book, at the 1984 Republican National Convention, Secretary of Transportation Elizabeth Hanford Dole and her husband, Senator Bob Dole, were mentioned as a possible husband-wife, president–vice-president team in the 1988 election.)

*But why might "teams" of lovers or married couples work out when more casual workplace liaisons have caused disruption?* There are several reasons. First, because neither would report to the other, they would have equal rank with no opportunity to exert favoritism, and the company would make them legitimate by institutionalizing their team role as an accepted option open to many people. It would not be an elite privilege for only a chosen few, nor would the team be seen as having more power than both people individually, although their productivity might be more than double. In terms of power, they would be seen as a unit, and might actually have less influence than two single people. And since the relationship would be out in the open, there would no longer be the need for secrets, cover-ups, or gossip.

Another idea, suggested by Marina Whitman, vice president of General Motors, would be a particular advantage for workers in general when lovers and couples operate together. Her thought was to have performance evaluations done by teams instead of individuals, "so that you don't have your future in one person's hands. It's not good for business, and it's not good for them." It would certainly allow a fairer and more objective evaluation of these man-woman units rather than leaving it to a supervisor who may not be very creative or imaginative or who may be biased against the idea of couple teams.

In one interesting experiment, Du Pont is offering a wide variety of seminars to improve their executive male-female relationships. To be sure they reach the concerns of both males and females, the company has employed a male-female consulting team from New Dynamics in Durham, New Hampshire. Seminars are conducted at corporate headquarters in Wilmington, Delaware, ten times a year for nine men and nine women who come from Du Pont offices around the country. Supervisors and their direct subordinates do not participate in the same program.

## FUTURE STRATEGIES AND ISSUES:
### THE DOUBLE GAP

I would like now to look at the larger picture. It seems that, fearing the repercussions of even discussing what it means to have women executives in the corporation, or not realizing the time has come to examine the subject closely and make policy changes, senior corporate officers have either ignored the matter or tried to sweep it out the door. Corporate mentality in this regard is lagging seriously behind the social realities, always a potentially dangerous situation. When people's freedoms are squelched and forbidden, it engenders revolutions. Actually, the revolution has begun and it is taking place both in the corporation, where employees hide and lie about their real lives, and in the courts, where they challenge the legality of corporate rules.

What the top officers need to address immediately is the conundrum I call the Double Gap. Two dangerous rifts threaten most corporations. One is the gap between the younger and older executives, and the other is the gap between the top officers and everybody else in the corporation. In both cases, large groups of people are not willing to listen to the sounds of change.

One senior vice president, after years of observing others around him, said, "The people at the top don't want to hear about this, don't want to waste their time on it. They have other things that are going to make money for them. Worrying about people is not normally the way you make money. The point is that in any business, the most important commodity is people, but almost nobody realizes it."

Whether the men at the top realize this or not, no one can deny the state of confusion that exists in general because not enough top officers are studying the effects of having women among their executives, or asking for appropriate ways of modernizing the corporate culture to accommodate them. As we have seen in instances of romantic involvement, some companies fire the woman, some fire the higher-powered man, some insist on transferring one of the parties, some don't allow affairs, some couldn't care less, some impose their morals and some don't, many worry about affairs if one or both people are married to others, some frown on all affairs, and some allow marriage among those within the corporation but will not allow a spouse to be hired from outside. Among romantically involved employees, some leave before being asked to find another job, others stay and are fired, some give up the romance and concentrate on their carrers, others fight a dismissal in court, some go to excruciating lengths to hide their romance, and still others assume that it is only their business and go on merrily enjoying having an affair or resulting marriage. Some find the presence of the opposite sex disturbing; others find it exciting and stimulating. Some men seem to be able to work well with women; others don't.

Who is going to bring clarity to all this disorder? Why aren't the top officers listening? Apparently there is a perception among many executives that a *number* of problems have failed to attract their attention. Polls show a continuing downturn in the belief of middle management in their top managers' ability. In an Opinion Research Corporation survey on supervision conducted over a period of years at 200 companies, 250,000 managers, line supervisors, and professionals complained of a sharp decline in "the willingness of management to listen." The study, called "Supervising in the 80's: Trends in Corporate America" and conducted by ORC vice presidents Dr. William A. Schiemann and Dr. Brian S. Morgan, asked about the willingness of management to listen to complaints and problems. In 1970, 54 percent of middle managers said top management was willing to listen. In 1979, the figure had fallen to 51 percent, and in 1984, to 46 percent.

The figures were even more dramatic with regard to the question "How do you rate your company on the ability of its top management?" Among middle managers in 1970, 69 percent had confidence in top management; by 1979, the number had dropped to 61 percent, and by 1984 it had plummeted to 47 percent. Similar declines were found among supervisors and professionals.

How can top management be made to listen, to instill confidence in their ability to understand and respond to the changing nature of corporate society? One big part of the answer is to have conferences of top executives to discuss the nature of executive interaction and what they, as corporate leaders, ought to be doing about it. As in every other facet of company operations, they should be leading. They should be sensitive to the fact that, as consultant Janice Eddy has observed, male bosses in their late thirties, early forties, and up are having difficulty managing the new young women in their twenties and early thirties who are really driving and more ambitious than the men. "Those women employees are out of sync with their bosses. Men are not used to managing aggressive, ambitious women," notes Eddy, "and the women tend to feel more qualified and don't feel they are being managed by men who are better or more competent than they are." It is up to the top management to work out ways of bridging the corporate generation gap.

With a similar sense of urgency, the top officers should turn their attention to a second area of noncommunication: the culture gap.

Dr. Ralph H. Kilmann of the University of Pittsburgh's Graduate School of Business has conducted many surveys which measure culture gap. He asked a number of managers and top executives to describe the unwritten rules that influence behavior in their organizations, such as:

"Don't rock the boat." "Cheat on your expense account." "Maintain the status quo." "Don't make waves." He then developed an instrument with norm pairs such as: "Don't disagree with your boss" versus "Always try to improve." "Don't disagree with your boss" versus "Disagree with your boss." "Don't mix friendship with business" versus "Mix friendship with business."

He asked the respondents to fill out the questionnaire in two ways: first, according to the actual norms operating in their organization; and second, according to what they thought the norms should be if they wanted to improve performance and morale. The difference between the two becomes the culture gap. In other words, it is the difference between the actual and the desired. Doing this in a number of corporations, Dr. Kilmann has discovered some very large culture gaps. "I think American industry has a serious culture problem and, for the most part, doesn't even know it.

"What I am finding," he stressed, "is that as you go higher up in the organization hierarchy, managers are unaware of the gap. It's as if they believe their own publicity. The top officers say, 'We reward innovation.' But the culture says, 'It doesn't pay to work hard or try to do something different. Keep things the same. We've been burned in the past.' Of course, the larger the gap, the more obstacles to performance, regardless of what the formal documents say."

It seems to me that this Culture Gap is likely to become the Organization Trap. It may explain why nothing is being done to understand the implications of having women executives in the corporation, and why the very thought of romance among their executives is anathema to the top officers. It may be true that they really don't *want* to hear anything about it, as many have suspected, because it's an emotional problem which they know nothing of and feel uncomfortable even thinking about. They are afraid of it enough to try to ignore it and, as Dr. Kilmann says, "to believe their own slogan: 'We know how to handle it.' "

Dr. Kilmann has worked with companies where the top executive group, the CEO, chairman of the board, and the top ten or twelve operating officers, didn't want to conduct a culture survey, and the reason, says Dr. Kilmann, was that "they didn't want to know what's going on. They wanted to be removed from it. They felt that if they didn't look at the problem it would go away."

He said in one case he was hired to conduct a three-day workshop on culture, and he suggested making a survey of that corporation's employees so that he would have something concrete to talk to them about. He was told, "No, we don't want to do this. We don't think the top group wants to hear the results. We don't want to surprise them." The alarming thing is that when he tells this story at other major corporations, they all say, "Is that our company you're talking about?" It sounds to them like their own senior officers.

The men at the top guide their companies, making decisions about adding new technologies, finding new markets, even approving dress codes and informing employees about what kind of attaché case fits the company image, but they won't deal with solving culture problems such as basic employee relationships, emotional interaction, or the emotional health of the employees—without whom they'd be out of business. Yet they direct their managers to step in and take action when a relationship surfaces, action that may often be illegal, unproductive, or bad business.

The main point of having executives is their value in the corporate setting. Whether or not they cheat on their spouses and have affairs has no direct effect on their value to the corporation, and no moral judgments should be made unless the company believes one of the purposes of its existence is to protect the sanctity of family life.

As I have noted earlier, if companies continue to fire increasing numbers of people in whom they have invested a lot of money, their executives are going to be leaving precisely at the point at which they have become valuable to the corporation. And the estimated loss of firing a middle manager is as much as $65,000.

Corporations, it would seem, are not always aware of the right issues:

- The issue corporation leaders must address is *not* how best to suppress romance, or how best to suppress sexual attraction. Both are impossible and foolhardy. The issue is how to help people manage themselves so that sexual attraction does not jeopardize their careers, but rather enhances them.
- The issue is recognizing that all the motives which have been causing corporations to fire, transfer, and harass people in romantic situations existed before women came, and were an accepted part of corporate life. Just because the sight of men and women together tends to be suggestive, it should not color a manager's judgment and cause him or her to react any differently than if two men were seen together.
- The issue is allowing employees to remain whole people rather than telling them to leave their humanity at home when they come to work. It is understanding that romance is part of being whole. And the more the corporation adheres to the "whole person" concept, the more dynamic the work environment will be.
- The issue is not forcing your employees to hide and be deceptive. An atmosphere where people have to lie is damaging to both the individual and the company because, as Dr. Macleod explains it, "When lies become accepted, lying becomes the norm. One lie begets another, and the lies and cover-ups can get more elaborate, and more destructive. It is much better that truth be the norm."
- The issue is establishing an adult atmosphere—the natural next step after the coed university, dorm, or busi-

ness school—where there will be coed networks and bisexual buddy systems. You can cow some of the people some of the time, but never all of the people any of the time, and those who refuse to be straitjacketed are growing in numbers.

- The issue is having an open, relaxed arrangement for counseling, seminars, and discussion groups where talking out the knots and bumps in an adult manner will decrease the tension between the sexes and the generations and allow employees to formulate their own private code of individual behavior which will work for them and their company.
- The issue is changing the atmosphere of the corporation from an all-male inner sanctum to a coed working situation where most of the men and women are *not* sleeping with each other (the presumption is not automatically made that they are) and where executive women are treated as executives first. A woman may use her sexual charm to gain a sale, but men use their masculine charm to do exactly the same thing. That's what salesmanship is all about. The sex of the charmer is irrelevant.
- The issue is creating a serious, constructive, yet tolerant atmosphere, and not one of suspicions, gossip, and fear where company spies go around checking license plates, addresses, and phone numbers to ferret out the live-in lovers. As one observer said, "Dress codes are enough. God forbid we should get into living codes."
- The issue is installing a program to enlighten management and help men, particularly older ones, feel comfortable working with women. It may be hard to get a budget that finances talk about sexual relations, but that is one of the things that should soon go into the corporate budget. It is no less important than stress, alcohol-

ism, drugs, and physical fitness. If ignored, it will become a dramatic problem.

- The issue is to stop treating office romance as though it were the black plague. One vice president said that of all the romances he knows of, 95 percent worked out well, and there were problems in only 5 percent, where people actually hurt their careers.

- The issue is that the makeup of the corporation's human stockpile is changing. The number of professionals is growing. There are many more of them than there are executives, and this particularly applies to women. Corporations simply cannot treat its professionals—its doctors, lawyers, psychologists, engineers, research scientists—like children. There has also been a great growth in service industries where executive-level men and women are computer programmers, word-processing supervisors, market analysts, statisticians, advertising-account specialists, management consultants—and none of these highly educated women or men can be subservient to an omnipotent employer with archaic standards and a narrow focus.

- The issue is that there is no longer one corporate morality designed by the man at the top. There are a great many individual moralities that count today, and they vary, just as people do.

- The issue is that you do not maximize profits by discarding human resources that now and then need a simple repair job, after investing a lot to find and develop them in the first place. If they are good, you should covet them.

- The issue is that if you are dictatorial in one area of human management, you will have dull, uniform, and predictable people when, in other areas, you want them to be bright, creative, innovative, and original. It won't work. You can't have it both ways.

The issue, in the end, is actively to speed change. Everything needs to move faster today, and it would be a wise decision to cut through the dead weight of old-fashioned norms by encouraging deviation.

What I mean is described in an experiment done at Swarthmore College in the 1950s. Three lines, A, B, and C, all of different lengths, were shown on a single card, to seven people who sat in a row. They were asked to indicate which of these three lines was identical in length to a fourth line, D, shown on a second card. One by one they indicated their choice. Although line D was, in fact, identical to line C, each of the first six persons, who were in on the experiment, indicated line D was similar to line A. Only the seventh person was the unknowing subject.

As each person answered in turn, this seventh subject became increasingly uneasy, anxious, and doubtful of his own perceptions. When it was his turn to respond, the seventh subject agreed with the group 40 percent of the time. When subjects were alone, their error rate was less than 1 percent.

Thus any group will have a strong influence on those who might deviate from it in thought or action. Because people need acceptance from others, they will often deny their own, more informed perceptions. The impact of the group on its members is, as the experiment proved, extremely powerful. The corporation, however, should open the way for its deviants (often its valuable innovators) to be heard, rather than to be gossiped about, shouted at, or punished, and that includes those with suggestions for normalizing the interaction between the men and women of the corporation.

As Sara Kiesler explains in her book *Interpersonal Processes in Groups and Organizations,* published in 1978, acceptable social interaction develops "as people in a group come to agree that certain beliefs are true and certain behaviors appropriate." This forces uniformity, holds a group together, helps individuals evaluate others and themselves, and is a way of getting social rewards such as liking and respect. However, she makes the point that sometimes there is an overreliance on norms and conventional wisdom rather than searching for new information. But although conformity provides a needed stability, it is deviance which is a source of growth. Says Kiesler, "a minority of people in groups function as pioneers in new behavioral territory by braving deviance and testing the value of ideas that defy acceptable ways of thinking," and it is this which leads to important innovation.

## A PERSONAL CODE

In most areas of our lives, the trend has been away from the strict ethics of the past—parental, religious, educational—and toward the extremely flexible standards which now guide so much of what we do. Yet despite this increasing permissiveness, there remain important parts of our society that have yet to be touched by more modern standards. The corporation, because it is one of the last outposts of male domination, is one of those areas where what is permissible among its male and female executives has not been adequately updated.

Though sweeping social changes have affected our mores, making it possible for men and women in greater numbers than ever to have affairs while married, to live together while unmarried, or to marry, divorce, and remarry serially, there are still those antiquated attitudes in the corporation, as we have seen, which hang on like barnacles. This puts business out of step with much of the rest of society. Bucking a trend which already has made itself part of modern life makes little sense.

The final step in the liberalization of rules governing male and female behavior, as far as the corporation is concerned, and one that seems inevitable, will have to be a state of enlightened self-supervision. As the rules of the past collapse because they are challenged, the final goal should be a situation where each individual will bear the responsibility of good judgment based on his or

241

her own personal code—a kind of self-imposed honor code.

In learning how to relate to the opposite sex in the office, whether romantically or while working together, the good executives, as one insurance officer described it, "will be the ones who can separate out their personal biases when necessary in order to make a decision that is of common good to the people affected. They are not gods, but somehow they will rise above the day-to-day emotionalism and make fairly rational decisions. That is a very important trait in a good executive. And individuals that can't do that are just not going to cut it."

As personal codes become the accepted model, the corporate culture will undergo this one last adjustment to fit in with larger social norms. And though it may surprise a number of top executives, the result will not be anarchy. Usually the more responsibility people have, the more honorable they become.

This is not to say that honor codes always work perfectly. Some people cheat. Some have never learned to control their emotions, and some have never grown up. Problems will appear. But there will be fewer problems and greater devotion to a corporation that allows its executives to direct their own lives. Nor is this to say that if people have love affairs, productivity will automatically increase, so that one will be able to measure the likelihood of profits by counting the number of romances. That would be to carry the notion of a liberated corporate culture from the sublime to the ridiculous.

But it is pretty obvious that people of both sexes who relate well to each other in any of a variety of intensities on a scale from friendship to love, who care about their work and their colleagues, and who are unfettered by old-fashioned, restrictive codes of conduct that squelch necessary interaction, will make life within the corporation more productive and profitable. For once, the organization will be seen as beneficent and compassionate.

Individual values and corporate values have often led in opposite directions, and sometimes people have had to give up some of their humanity to earn the big bucks they needed to live on, or leave the corporation altogether. In the Northeast, for example, the states of Maine, Vermont, and New Hampshire are filled with men who fled the corporate hand that tried to squeeze the blood and spirit out of them.

It is time the individual and business joined forces to create one set of values in *all* corporate cultures, one that is receptive to new ideas, and adaptable enough to allow its men and women executives to express their whole personalities in a wide range of human relationships from shared interests to friendship to romance. If corporations persist in building walls, people will continue to try to climb over them.

# ACKNOWLEDGMENTS

$\mathcal{T}$he idea for *Corporate Romance* was suggested by my former husband, Clay S. Felker, who has continued to be a source of journalistic inspiration, as he has been for so many other writers. I, and they, have benefited from his genius for spotting new trends before they have even surfaced. He is a good friend and much, much more, and I thank him heartily for leading the way for me.

My deepest appreciation to my editor, Elisabeth Scharlatt. She is the author's dream of the concerned editor. She quite simply cares, helps, edits, encourages. I have benefited enormously from her editorial skill.

Grateful thanks to my agent, Mel Sokolow, who, between trips to California and the squash courts, managed to find a home for this book.

I am indebted also to Bob Levine, whose critical eye, relentless humor, and editorial suggestion helped speed the book along its way.

Profound thanks to a special person and my dear friend, Theodore Stagg, Jr., whose continual and unwavering emotional support helped to propel me onward. His strength and positiveness illumined all the difficult days.

Thanks also to historian Betsy Gilliam. She offered friendship and a necessary respite on afternoons when we both left our desks to walk and talk and find sanity in the lonely job of writing.

And to Dr. Richard Robbins, a delightful friend, excellent cook, and solver of problems—human as well as opthalmological—my gratitude for his good talk during this period.

# CORPORATE ROMANCE

Grateful recognition for his trust to Steve Taylor, a reporter for the *Peninsula Times Tribune* in Redwood City, California, who believed a fellow journalist he'd never heard of until the moment of her phone call enough to spend time and his own money to help retrieve information for her.

My thoughts still remain with editor Fred Hills, whose initial probing questions sparked my formulation of how the research would go.

A rousing chorus of esteem for the men and women executives whose perceptions of what was going on around them in the corporation made my interviews with them so valuable. Although they asked for anonymity, I knew their names and companies, yet they trusted me with their personal stories because they wanted this book to be written. Without their interest and help, it would have been very difficult to document attitudes among males and females in business today, and the problems they have in relating to each other.

Love and thanks to my inventive son, Geoffrey W. Aldridge, who helped me give up my favorite, outdated typewriter. He pushed me into the future by teaching me enough to write this book on our computer, and by solving all the problems I encountered when the machine would not obey.

To my friend, sociologist Marvin Bressler, profound gratitude for his generosity with time and his witty, usually brilliant comments on the riddle of human nature—all given to me when I needed it most.

And blessings to Sally Kunstadter, who cured me of the post-book *blahs* in her heavenly house by the sea.

Lastly, a super embrace for my husband, Charles F. Westoff, who will always interrupt his own projects to answer my questions, give his judgment, and untangle my dilemmas. He is a first-rate editor despite the fact that he is a demographer. We've been through a lot of books together.